SPITFIRE AT WAR: 2

SPITFIRE
AT WAR: 2

ALFRED PRICE

LONDON
IAN ALLAN LTD

First published 1985

ISBN 0 7110 1511 2

Published by Ian Allan Ltd, Shepperton, Surrey;
and printed by Ian Allan Printing Ltd at their works
at Coombelands in Runnymede, England

Contents

Introduction

In assembling material for *Spitfire at War 2* I have tried to repeat the formula which proved successful with *Spitfire at War:* namely, to describe a series of incidents, and to present little-known historical documents which will interest those reading about the aircraft for the first time, while adding to the knowledge of enthusiasts possessing other books on the subject. And to back this with a large number of unpublished or rarely seen photographs which will please even the most expert reader.

The first chapter, 'K5054: A Mystery Resolved', presents recently uncovered evidence on the date of the first flight of the Spitfire, for which the author is grateful to Hugh Scrope, Secretary of the Vickers company. When designing the Spitfire, Reginald Mitchell and his team went to considerable lengths to produce an airframe that was clean aerodynamically and as light as possible. 'A Very Efficient Fighter' gives drag and weight analyses for the main components of the Spitfire to show how successful the designers were. For any pilot the first combat missions on which he encounters the enemy are fraught with danger, as he learns the art of survival

in the hardest school of all. In 'Baptism of Fire' Colin Gray tells of one of his early combat missions covering the evacuation of British troops from Dunkirk in May 1940, which he was lucky to survive. In war some units will achieve successes with few losses, other will lose aircraft and pilots so rapidly that they have to be pulled out of the fight after a few days. In 'Thirteen Days in August' Dennis Armitage tells the story of No 266 Squadron during the Battle of Britain, and how the unit suffered so heavily that it had to be withdrawn from action after only 13 days in the south of England. After the Battle of Britain, daylight air combats became a rarity over the home counties. 'Skirmish Over Kent' describes the meeting between Trevor Gray in a Spitfire and Helmut Fischer in a Messerschmitt 110 reconnaissance aircraft in December 1940, and how the two pilots were brought together by this author nearly 40 years later. By 1942 Fighter Command was sending Spitfires deep into occupied Europe. Pilots had to learn the art of handling their engines so they could cruise at high speed and react quickly if they were 'bounced' by enemy fighters; but they had to do so without burning fuel at too high a rate. 'Correct Engine Handling – Key to Survival' tells how it was done. Also in 1942 the Spitfire fighters were sent to defend Malta. In 'Besieged on Malta' George Hows tells of his experiences as a ground crewman with No 1453 Squadron. The Seafire, the deck-landing version of the Spitfire, first went into service with the Royal Navy in 1942 but from the start there were

Spitfires flying past a clip-winged Mk V of No 401 Squadron, RCAF, at Biggin Hill in September 1943. *Public Archives of Canada*

difficulties operating it from aircraft carriers. Jeffrey Quill, the Chief Test Pilot of Supermarine, wrote a lucid report on the difficulties and how they could be overcome, which is given in full in 'Problems with the Seafire'. During the war Spitfires served with numerous foreign air arms including the US Army Air Forces. In 'With the Eighth Air Force to Berlin' Walt Weitner of the US 14th Photo Squadron tells of the reconnaissance mission he flew to the German capital in a Spitfire, following the first large scale daylight bombing attack on the city in March 1944. Despite the efforts of the Air Sea Rescue service, during World War 2 pilots unfortunate enough to be forced down in the sea even close to land had no certainty they would be rescued. John Saffery tells of the difficulties he experienced after he baled out into the sea from his Spitfire in 'Anyway, it is only a Short Sea Crossing'. During the closing months of the war no part of German occupied Europe was beyond the reach of Spitfires. In 'Spitfires Over the Balkans' David Green tells of the operations by his squadron over Yugoslavia. Spitfires were flown by pilots of more than a score of nationalities, and introduced 'flying English' into their respective languages. 'Franglais for Spitfire Pilots' shows the impact this had on No 349 (Belgian) Squadron. In the late war period Supermarine developed and tested the Spiteful, intended as a replacement for the Spitfire in Royal Air Force fighter squadrons. Although orders were placed the aircraft never went into full production, however, and in 'Test Flying the Spiteful' Pat Shea-Simonds explains why.

As well as those named above, the author would particularly like to express his thanks to the following for making available material and photographs used in this book: Jay Spenser at the Smithsonian Institution in Washington, Peter Arnold, Carl Geust, Paul Lambermont, The Royal Air Force Museum, the Imperial War Museum, The Public Archives of Canada, Air Marshal Sir Geoffrey Tuttle, Grp Capt Alan Wright, Gordon Green, John Saffery, Harry van der Meer, Christopher Elliott and Jim Oughton.

Until the end of 1942 all Royal Air Force aircraft mark numbers were given in roman numerals. From 1943 to 1948 new aircraft entering service carried arabic mark numbers while the older types carried roman mark numbers. As a convention in this book Spitfire and Seafire marks up to XVI are given in roman numerals and those of later versions are given in arabic numerals.

Previous books on the Spitfire have contained lengthy accounts of the development of the aircraft, and rather than repeat these this book concentrates on less known parts of the aircraft's history. readers requiring detail on the evolution of the Spitfire through its various marks should refer to the author's book *The Spitfire Story* (Janes, 1982), accepted at the most comprehensive work on this aspect of the aircraft.

Those who flew, serviced or built Spitfires, or are interested in their story, might like to know to know of the existence of The Spitfire Society, formed to perpetuate the memory of this most famous of all fighting aircraft. Those wishing to know more should contact Grp Capt David Green RAF (Rtd), The Chairman, The Spitfire Society, R. J. Mitchell Hall, Kingsbridge Lane, Southampton SO1 0GB.

Alfred Price
Uppingham
Rutland

Spitfire IXs of No 411 Squadron RCAF at Heesch, Holland in March 1945.
Public Archives of Canada

1

K5054: A Mystery Resolved

Although the Spitfire is, arguably, the most successful fighting aircraft ever produced, some aspects of the history of its design and development have been difficult to establish with accuracy. The Supermarine company saw itself as a builder of aircraft rather than a keeper of records, and many of the prewar records it did keep were destroyed when the works was bombed in September 1940. As a result historians and writers attempting to assemble accounts on the evolution of the Spitfire have been forced to rely on secondary sources of information, personal memories and published accounts, which in many cases have been proved unreliable and which tend to perpetuate errors already made.

Even the date of the first flight of the prototype Spitfire, K5054, has been a matter for discussion. Some published accounts stated it was on 5 March 1936, others said the historic event took place on the following day. In a previous book (*The Spitfire Story*, Janes, 1982) this author reviewed the available evidence on the date of the first flight. In spite of an intensive search he had been able to secure no direct evidence written at the time or soon afterwards to support either date; the evidence available was either implicit, or else

it had been recorded so long after the event that it could not be considered reliable. On balance, the meagre evidence available seemed to point to the prototype having made its maiden flight on 6 March 1936.

Having searched long and fruitlessly to resolve the mystery, this author is extremely grateful to Mr Hugh Scrope of the Vickers company for the hardest piece of evidence he has yet seen on the date of the first flight of the Spitfire. The evidence takes the form of an accounts sheet prepared for the board of Vickers, the parent company, of expenditure by its Supermarine subsidiary on 'Modified Single-Seater Fighter K5054'. The document noted that up to 29 February 1936 a total of £14,637 had been spent on the aircraft which had yet to fly.

On 2 April 1936 the board of Vickers met at Weybridge and the accounts sheet was presented. But beforehand Henry Duvall, the Company Secretary, had added a handwritten note to the sheet giving the latest cost of the new fighter as '£15,000 app', below which he noted that it 'Flew on 5 Mar 36'. From the minutes of the meeting we know that Reginald Mitchell was one of those who attended; he was a stickler for detail and it is unlikely in

K5054, the prototype Spitfire, pictured at Eastleigh in May 1936, shortly after it had been painted in its light-blue colour scheme. *Smith*

Statement of accounts submitted to the meeting of the Board of Directors of Vickers Ltd on 2 April 1936, which mentioned that K5054 had flown on 5 March. In spite of an intensive search, this is the only direct evidence the author has seen concerning the date of the historic first flight of this aircraft.

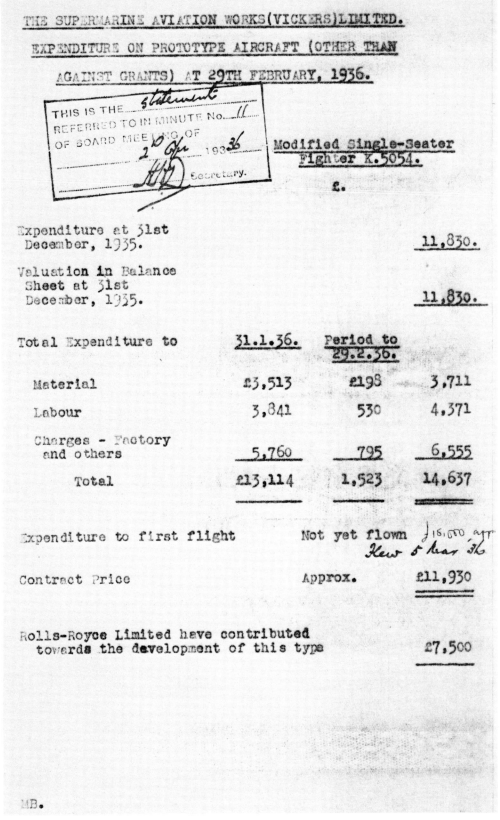

THE SUPERMARINE AVIATION WORKS (VICKERS) LIMITED.

EXPENDITURE ON PROTOTYPE AIRCRAFT (OTHER THAN

AGAINST GRANTS) AT 29TH FEBRUARY, 1936.

THIS IS THE _Statement_
REFERRED TO IN MINUTE No. _11_
OF BOARD MEETING OF
2 Apr 193_6_
[signature] Secretary.

Modified Single-Seater
Fighter K.5054.

£.

	31.1.36.	Period to 29.2.36.	
Expenditure at 31st December, 1935.			11,830.
Valuation in Balance Sheet at 31st December, 1935.			11,830.
Total Expenditure to			
Material	£3,513	£198	3,711
Labour	3,841	530	4,371
Charges - Factory and others	5,760	795	6,555
Total	£13,114	1,523	14,637

Expenditure to first flight   Not yet flown _£15,000 apx_
Flew 5 Mar '36

Contract Price   Approx.   £11,930

Rolls-Royce Limited have contributed
towards the development of this type   £7,500

MB.

the extreme that he would have let pass an incorrect date of the maiden flight of his new fighter.

Although it makes only a passing reference to the first flight of K5054, in historical terms the new piece of evidence is extremely strong. Duvall would certainly have known when the first flight took place, his note was penned within a month of that date and had he got it wrong the error would certainly have been pointed out at the time and corrected. There is now little room for doubt that the date of the maiden flight of K5054, the prototype Spitfire, was 5 March 1936.

Above left:
K5054, the prototype Spitfire, pictured at Eastleigh in May 1936, shortly after it had been painted in its light-blue colour scheme. *Smith*

Left:
The prototype seen in February 1937 at Martlesham Heath, about to begin air firing trials of its eight .303in Browning guns.
RAF Museum

Below:
The prototype at Eastleigh, fitted with ejector exhausts and camouflaged; this photograph was taken some time after September 1937. *Smith*

2
A Very Efficient Fighter

K9787, the first production
Spitfire, with Jeffrey Quill at
the controls, pictured during
its maker's trials near
Southampton in May 1938.
The drag and weight figures
given below refer to the
aircraft in the configuration
shown.
RAF Museum/Charles Brown

The most notable external feature of the Spitfire, apart from its beautiful lines, is the aerodynamic cleanliness of its airframe. The table which follows gives the drag analysis of the airframe of the Spitfire I, measured in pounds at a notional speed of 100ft/sec. In each case the figures are very low for an aircraft of this period.

Profile Drag	*pounds*
Wings	20.3
Fuselage	7.3
Tailplane, Fin and Rudder	4.6
Effect of Camouflage Paint	1.5
Total Profile Drag	33.7
Induced Drag	
Lift	2.4
Washout	0.6
Total Induced Drag	3.0
Cooling Drag	
Glycol Radiator	6.0
Oil Radiator	1.0
Air Intake	1.0
Total Cooling Drag	8.0
Miscellaneous	
Controls	1.2
Windscreen	1.2
Tail Wheel	2.0
Wing/Body Interference	1.5
Aerial Post	0.2
Gun Holes	0.5
Rivets and Joints	0.5
Total Miscellaneous	7.1
Not Accounted For	8.4
TOTAL DRAG OF AEROPLANE	**60.2**

Above:
K9787 pictured soon after delivery to Martlesham Heath for service testing, August 1938.

Left and Overleaf:
These early Mk Is are pictured at the refuelling point at Eastleigh, January 1939. K9846 was the 60th production aircraft. K9849 is being readied for engine runs with several components still to be fitted; note the serial number chalked on the fuselage. *Flight*

As well as being clean aerodynamically, the airframe of the Spitfire was a highly efficient structure in engineering terms. By meticulous attention to the design of each item, Reginald Mitchell and his team were able to produce an aircraft that was strong enough to perform all reasonable combat manoeuvres – and a lot of unreasonable ones. And, as can be seen from the weight break-down of the Spitfire I which follows, this strength was not achieved for an inordinate weight penalty:

Structure	*pounds*
Wings	820
Engine Cowling	86
Engine Mounting	58
Fuselage and Fin	426
Tailplane and Elevator	58
Rudder	18
Tail Wheel	28
Wheels and Brakes	90
Chassis and Retracting Gear	192
Controls	91
Accommodation	23
Total Structure	1,890
Power Plant	
Engine	1,412
Airscrew Hub	36
Wooden Airscrew and Spinner	96
Ejector Exhausts	30
Engine Accessories and Piping	61
Radiator	98
Cooling System	56
Cooling Fluid	142
Petrol Tanks	57
Oil Tanks	47
Total Power Plant	2,035
Load Carried	
Pilot and Parachute	200
Military Load (guns, ammunition, gunsight, etc)	685
Petrol (84 gallons)	646
Oil (six gallons)	54
Total Load Carried	1,585
Sundries Unaccounted for	335
Stressing Allowance	30
TOTAL WEIGHT	**5,875**

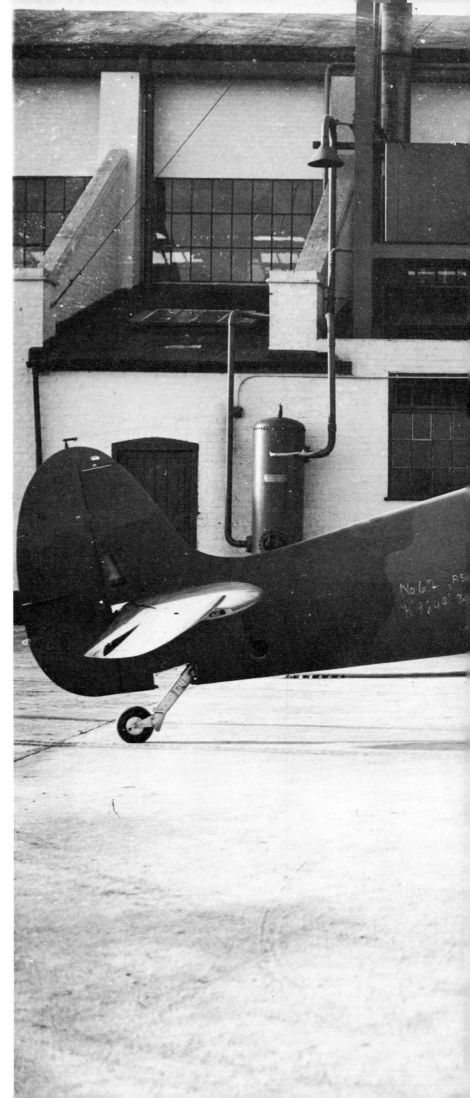

Right:
K9798, the 11th production Spitfire, pictured after a landing accident at Duxford in April 1939 while serving with No 19 Squadron. *Cozens*

Far right:
A pair of Mk Is of No 66 Squadron being refuelled at Duxford during the early war period. Although concentrating aircraft in this way made servicing easier, the first attacks on airfields would teach the RAF the value of dispersal.

Below:
Mk Is of No 611 Squadron pictured during a scramble take-off from Digby in Lincolnshire, January 1940. Note the small wing and fuselage roundels and the lack of fin flash, standard at this time. *Flight*

3

Baptism of Fire

During the so-called 'Phoney War', the period prior to the opening of the German offensive in the West on 10 May 1940, Spitfires had occasionally been in action against German bombers operating off the coasts of England and Scotland. But they did not encounter enemy fighters until, a few days after the offensive began, Allied troops were forced to withdraw within range of the Spitfire squadrons based in southern England. During the final week of May and the beginning of June, Royal Air Force Fighter Command endeavoured to cover the evacuation of Allied troops from Dunkirk. In the course of these operations Spitfires found themselves in action against enemy fighters of equivalent performance for the first time; now the Royal Air Force's premier fighter type had to show that it could take punishment, as well as dish it out.

Plt Off Colin Gray, a New Zealander flying Spitfires with No 54 Squadron based at Hornchurch, first went into action on 24 May against an enemy formation near Calais and was credited with one Messerschmitt 109 damaged. On the following day his unit escorted a squadron of Fleet Air Arm Swordfish attacking German ground troops advancing east of Dunkirk. The lumbering biplanes and their escorts reached the target without interference from enemy fighters, completed their attack and turned back for England. As their charges headed out to sea with no enemy aircraft in sight the Spitfires, freed of the requirement to escort them further, headed south looking for trouble. They soon found it, and in the action that followed Colin Gray's inexperience almost cost him his life.

'Suddenly we found ourselves in amongst a gaggle of 109's. I opened fire at one of them, but stopped when I noticed smoke coming back over my wings. That shook me – I thought somebody was firing at me. I pulled round hard but there was nobody there – what I had seen was cordite smoke blowing back from my own guns. I looked back at the Messerschmitt and saw Sgt John Norwell on its tail and the German pilot baling out.'

Afterwards Norwell and Gray were each credited with a half share in the destruction

of the Messerschmitt, but as the German fighter plunged earthwards Gray allowed his gaze to follow his falling enemy too long. The error nearly cost him his life.

'Suddenly there was one Hell of a row, like somebody running a bar along a piece of corrugated iron. The stick was knocked out of my hand and ended up in the left hand corner of the cockpit, and my aircraft flicked into a spiral dive. I grabbed the stick and hauled back on it, the Spitfire responded immediately and started to climb. I looked behind but didn't see anyone, the German pilot had not repeated my mistake of following me down. I selected 12 pounds [emergency boost] and continued my climb; the airspeed indicator read 240mph and I thought "This is bloody marvellous!" [the normal speed for a Spitfire in a steep climb was about 190mph indicated]. But then, as I continued the climb, the Spitfire began to shudder and it seemed as if it was going to stall. I couldn't understand it – the airspeed indicated still read 240mph. I eased the stick forwards, but still it read 240mph . . . Then I realised what had happened: my pitot head had been shot away, the needle had dropped to the 240mph position on the dial under gravity . . .

'I levelled out and took stock of the situation. One cannon shell had gone through the port aileron, that was what had knocked the stick out of my hand and sent the aircraft into the violent spiral dive which shook off the Messerschmitt. The airspeed indicator was out and there was no air pressure or hydraulic pressure, which meant that I had no flaps or brakes and I couldn't lower the undercarriage using the main hydraulic system. As I approached Hornchurch I blew down the undercarriage using the emergency carbon dioxide system, and saw the "undercarriage down" sticks push up through the wings and two green lights come on to indicate that the wheels were down and locked.

'The landing was very difficult. With the flaps up one came in at a different attitude than usual and, of course, I had no idea of my airspeed (the indicator still read 240mph!). The first time, I came in too fast. The station commander at Hornchurch, Wing Commander "Daddy" Bouchier, was watching my performance and was overheard to say "The silly young bugger, he's going too fast. He'll never get in!" He was right. I got my wheels almost on the ground, realised I was not going to make it and took off again. The second time I stood well back from the airfield, and dragged the aircraft in at just above stalling speed. That time I landed, and as I touched down the elevator cable finally parted and the control column collapsed back into my stomach.

'On examination of the Spitfire afterwards it was found that a cannon shell had gone through the inspection hatch in the rear fuselage and exploded inside. Splinters from the shell had slashed their way out of the skinning, leaving it looking like a cheese grater. The air bottles had been knocked out, so were the batteries. There were bullet holes up and down the fuselage and, of course, the cannon shell through the aileron. From the entry and exit holes of the bullets it was clear the Messerschmitt had dived on me from the right and above; it had been a very neat piece of deflection shooting.

'The Spitfire was put up on trestles and people from Vickers were invited to come and look at it, to see how much it had suffered. It was the first Hornchurch aircraft that had been fairly well clobbered, and still got back. Soon there would be many others.'

Colin Gray went on to become one of the most successful RAF fighter pilots of World War 2 and ended the conflict as a Wing Commander credited with $27\frac{1}{2}$ aerial victories. Yet of the many actions in which he fought, for him the most memorable was that on 25 May 1940 when lack of experience so nearly put a premature end to his career as a combat pilot.

No 92 Squadron Spitfires, photographed in May 1940 during the operations over Dunkirk when the unit still used the original GR code letters.

Top:
Aircraft GR-G, serial P9372. *Wright*

Above:
Plt Off Robert Stanford Tuck boarding his aircraft; note that the underside of the port wing had been painted black, standard at this time to provide a means of identification. *Wright*

Left:
Plt Off A. Wright with his aircraft GR-S; note the dimensions of the fuselage roundel. *Wright*

4

Thirteen Days in August

Somewhat the worse for wear, a Spitfire I of No 266 Squadron (unit code UO) is photographed taxying in to its dispersal at Wittering in September 1940 after the unit returned from operations in the south of England. Note the paint peeling off the fuselage roundel. The square patch on the top of the port wing was light-green gas-detecting paint. *via Forder*

The Battle of Britain in the summer of 1940 is the action which most readily springs to mind whenever the name 'Spitfire' is mentioned. In this account Dennis Armitage, at the time a Flight Lieutenant and junior Flight Commander with No 266 Squadron, gives his memories of the great air battle.

During the initial stages of the battle the Squadron was based at Wittering in the Midlands as part of No 12 Group, and saw little action. For the unit the period of quiet came to an abrupt end during the early morning darkness of 9 August, when it received orders that at first light it was to move to Northolt for a short detachment. Led by Sqn Ldr Rodney Wilkinson, 12 Spitfires took off from Wittering at 06.00hrs and headed south. On the way the weather deteriorated, however, with banks of low cloud concealing the ground. Unable to find Northolt, the Squadron headed back north until there was a break in the overcast and put down at the first airfield it came to, at Hatfield.

'This was most sporting because someone had thought of the brilliant idea of stringing quantities of barbed wire up and down the aerodrome. At that time Hatfield was used for ground training only, except for occasional test-flights by de Havillands, and the idea of the barbed wire was that it would upset any airborne divisions which might arrive from Germany. But in practice it was amazingly ineffective. Even with Spitfires, a machine which was notoriously nose-heavy on the ground, only one of the first section to land up-ended; and even that, I think, was due to a feeling that there was something peculiar about those yards of barbed wire trailing behind which caused the pilot to make a too sudden application of the brakes [Sgt A. Eade in L1059; the aircraft suffered Category 2 damage]. After that and a few belated red Verey lights, hundreds of small boys appeared – cadets who were doing their ground training and had been hurriedly kicked out of bed – and stood in two great lines to mark out a "secret" landing run which had been left clear for de Havillands, and the rest of us plonked down one at a time without further incident.

'It was still only 6.30am but someone rustled up some breakfast for us and over this we had a good healthy argument, which our C.O. won in the end, about whether anyone had thought of sending out warning signals about the barbed wire. By 8 o'clock the clouds had cleared and we flew on to Northolt, refuelled and settled down to wait. We were told we should return home at 3pm; at 3 we were told to wait till 5; at 5 to wait till 6; and at 6 o'clock we were told to take off for Tangmere.

'The eleven of us – the twelfth man, of course, had been left behind at Hatfield –

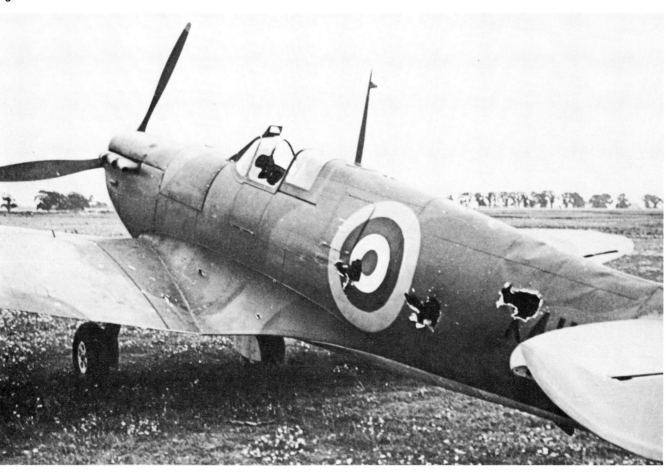

arrived there without further incident. We parked our aircraft, arranged to borrow ground-crews from a Hurricane squadron stationed there, fed, had a drink or two and so to bed – pyjamaless.'

No 266 Squadron's Spitfires remained at Tangmere for the next two days, during which its ground personnel arrived from Wittering. No sooner had the unit collected itself together than orders came in to prepare for yet another move, to Eastchurch on the 12th.

'The C.O., the Senior Flight Commander and myself were summoned to a most secret meeting. We were informed that we had been given special duties escorting Battles [bombers] across the Channel to bomb concentrations of "E-boats" which were now assembling along the French and Dutch coasts. It sounded horrid for the lads in the slow and aged Battles although not so bad for us. We were to operate from Eastchurch, on the Isle of Sheppey in the Thames Estuary, which would be ready for us the next day.

'In the meantime, in view of the greatly increased activity around Portsmouth, we might be called on to patrol the aerodrome if necessary but under no circumstances were we to engage the enemy if we could possibly avoid it – they wanted to be sure there would be a full squadron to go to Eastchurch next day.'

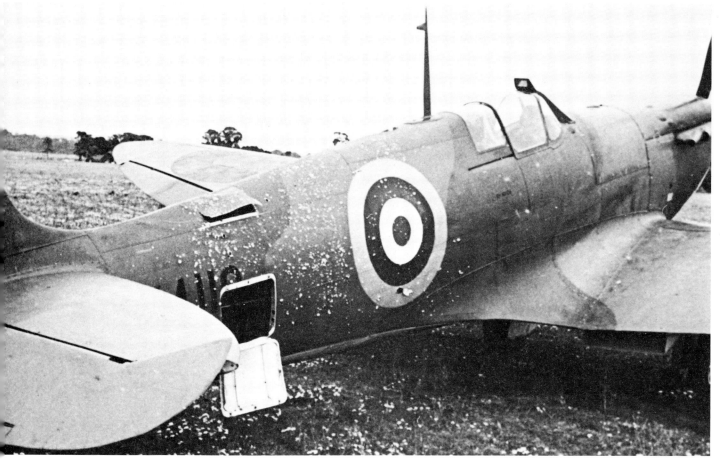

Plt Off Bob Doe of No 234 Squadron, one of the top-scoring RAF pilots during the Battle of Britain, credited with 15 victories. *Doe*

The orders to keep out of action were smartly superseded a couple of hours later, when a large force of Junkers 88's of Kampfgeschwader 51 attacked Portsmouth at mid-day. No 266 Squadron scrambled 12 Spitfires and in the action that followed it claimed four enemy aircraft destroyed, two probably destroyed and nine damaged. Two of its Spitfires were lost and one pilot, Plt Off Dennis Ashton, killed. After refuelling at Tangmere, the unit's remaining aircraft took off for Eastchurch as planned.

'We arrived at Eastchurch to find two squadrons of Battles and another half squadron of Spitfires [No 19] had arrived earlier that day, and after dinner Flight Commanders and above were summoned to a conference of war in the Group Captain's office.

'We were told the general scheme and apparently only two things were lacking. One was a special information service which was going to tell us where to find the fruitiest targets, and the other snag was that [the Battles] had not got any bombs. However, the G/C had reason to hope that both these things would be added unto us by after lunch the next day and in the meantime he suggested we might all have a really good night's rest – breakfast at 9.30am and another conference about 10 o'clock. It was actually 7.05 hours when the first bomb arrived. Not ours!'

The attack on Eastchurch was carried out by Dornier 17s of Kampfgeschwader 2 and caused severe damage to the airfield buildings. No 266 Squadron lost one airman killed, and one officer and five airmen injured. One of its Spitfires suffered damage.

'We held a brief council of war and decided to station six Spitfire pilots permanently in their machines. Until the raid we had every reason to expect we should get warning of the approach of the Luftwaffe – why we did not we never discovered – but there was no radio station at Eastchurch and our own R/T sets were, of course, no use until we were airborne, so with the telephone wires down communications were sticky.

'Fortunately the [other] aircraft were practically undamaged, but unfortunately all of our spare ammunition boxes had gone up with our hangar where they were stored – fully loaded, incidentally, which had all helped to make the fire interesting'.

On the following day, 14 August, the Squadron moved to Hornchurch.

15 August was one of the hardest-fought days of the Battle of Britain and No 266 Squadron was heavily engaged. The unit claimed three enemy aircraft destroyed and one damaged but lost two pilots killed, Plt Off F. Cale and Sgt F. Hawley. Armitage himself had a very narrow escape and suffered leg injuries:

'There had been the usual shemozzle which had eventually sorted itself out into one or two Spits, and three or four 109's buzzing round in tight circles, and I had just had the pleasure of seeing the three that I had been closeted with diving down towards the sea with one of them smoking nicely. Another

"possible", perhaps even a "probable", but not a "confirmed" because I was not silly enough to follow him down in case there was another waiting for me up in the sun – and there was. I have no idea how he slipped under my tail, but suddenly I heard a loud bang, something hit me in the leg, and there was a fearful noise of rushing air. Under these circumstances one's reactions are automatic, even though one has no idea what the Dickens has happened. I whipped into a vertical turn, looking fearfully up towards the blazing sun and then, as confidence returned, I spotted what was probably the cause of the trouble diving away, already some 5,000ft below. I realised that the noise was simply due to my perspex hood having been blown out and, that apart, my machine seemed quite manageable. My left leg was quite numb from the calf down; I put my hand down gingerly to feel if my foot was still there and, reassured on this point, I headed for home.

'On landing I found a cannon shell had exploded inside the fuselage, the spent head of the shell having found its way under the armour plating behind the seat and struck me on the leg. One of the elevator control wires was hanging on by a single thread and another cannon shell had just caught my port wing tip.'

The next day, 16 August, was even worse for No 266 Squadron. During a frenzied combat with Messerschmitt 109s near Canterbury Sqn Ldr Wilkinson, Sub Lt Greenshields (a Fleet Air Arm officer seconded to the RAF) and

Plt Off Bower were all killed; Flt Lt S. Bazley, the senior Flight Commander, baled out with burns; Plt Off Sodden was injured and his Spitfire wrecked during a crash landing; and one aircraft was damaged. One enemy aircraft was claimed destroyed and three probably destroyed.

In the course of just two days' fighting the unit had lost its three senior officers and five other pilots killed or injured; seven Spitfires had been destroyed and two damaged. Dennis Armitage, as senior surviving officer on the Squadron, had to take charge. With his engineering warrant officer he surveyed the damaged Spitfires in the hangar, amongst them the one in which he had been injured.

'One of the E.O.'s pet rules was the one about non-cannibalisation of aircraft. Many a time we had waited and waited with three or four unserviceable machines in the hangar, when all but one could have been put into the air by pinching the necessary parts from the remaining machine. But now things were different; we went to any lengths to get a machine flying again, patching and making-do in a thousand ways. And our straight-backed E.O. did not hesitate to cast aside his life-long principles, though I think it still hurt him to do so. And incidentally, for a whole month, he himself worked from dusk till dawn without a break, and most of the daylight hours as well.

'The jagged hole in the fuselage was nearly a foot in diameter. The E.O. shook his head and with one accord our eyes strayed towards another machine in the hangar with a badly

damaged starboard wing. I nodded and he nodded – no words passed but I knew that the starboard wing, the only undamaged part of my airframe, would be transferred by dawn.'

On the evening of 17 August No 266 Squadron took delivery of seven new Spitfires to make up the aircraft lost during the previous two days' fighting. There were no replacement pilots, however, and by now the unit was desperately short. Despite his injured leg Dennis Armitage had to lead the Squadron in the air as well as on the ground.
'My leg was very stiff and I had to hobble about with the aid of a stick and be helped into my Spit, but once there I was all right. Fortunately there is no place other than bed where full use of the legs is so unimportant as in an aeroplane.'

The restoration of No 266 Squadron to its full complement of aircraft brought only temporary relief, for on the next day the unit was again hit hard.
On the afternoon of 18 August the Squadron was involved in a skirmish with Me 109s near the coast and claimed one enemy aircraft destroyed, one probably destroyed and one damaged. Afterwards Dennis Armitage led his 11 Spitfires in to land at Manston to refuel and re-arm. No sooner had the last of the aircraft landed, however, than the airfield was strafed by 16 Me 109s of Jagdgweschwader 52. The commander watched as Sgt Don Kingaby had a narrow escape:
'He was the last but one to land and seeing the German fighters diving on him began to run for cover, but tripped and fell. Then for a few breathless seconds he rolled along the

ground with the bullets kicking up the earth not a foot away as the German tried to swing his aircraft to get his sights on.'

A bullet nicked one of Kingaby's fingers and another of the pilots suffered shock, but those were the only injuries suffered by the Squadron. Its Spitfires were less fortunate. Two were set on fire and burned out ('it's amazing how fiercely an aluminium aircraft will burn if it once gets going') and six others suffered damage. Of the 11 aircraft that had taken off from Hornchurch that morning only three returned in the afternoon.

On 19 August the weather broke and for the next five days there were no large scale air operations over southern England. On the 21st, having seen no further action, the Squadron received orders to withdrew north to Wittering to re-form. During its time in the south of England the unit had seen intensive action on four separate days and claimed nine enemy aircraft destroyed, six probably destroyed and 11 damaged. But in the achieving this it had lost six pilots killed (including the commander) and five wounded (including both flight commanders), out of the 19 pilots on strength at the beginning of the period. Twelve of its Spitfires were destroyed and eight damaged. For No 266 Squadron, it had been a very unlucky 13 days in August.

5
Skirmish Over Kent

By the third week in December 1940 the hard-fought daylight actions of the Battle of Britain were at an end. To counter the threat of attack by enemy fighters-bombers on London, pairs of squadrons of Spitfires now flew standing patrols over Kent during the daylight hours. But as autumn drew to an end the Luftwaffe appeared to have abandoned even this form of attack. Now enemy air incursions by day over southern England were restricted mainly to reconnaissance aircraft trying to sneak through the defences to photograph targets. Flying fast, high and alone, these aircraft presented difficult and fleeting targets. To catch them the Spitfire squadrons had to expend a disproportionate effort, as can be seen from the attempt on the morning of 21 December 1940 . . .

At 10.35hrs that morning there were blue skies over much of the south of England as No 64 Squadron based at Hornchurch received orders to put up a dozen Spitfires to mount a standing patrol in the Maidstone area. One of the squadron's pilots, Plt Off Trevor Gray, later told the author:
'After taking off from Hornchurch we flew to the so-called Maidstone patrol line which ran from Maidstone to the south coast. Once in position we patrolled at 15,000ft, the maximum we could sustain without using up our limited oxygen. Then it was a case of waiting for the enemy to come to us, but there was very little activity at this time.'

Five minutes after Gray and his comrades were airborne, the No 11 Group controller ordered a further dozen Spitfires, from No 611 Squadron based at Southend, to join them at the patrol line. One Spitfire was forced to return early with engine trouble but the remaining 23 aircraft flew up and down the patrol line in separate formations, engines throttled back to conserve fuel.

This was the position at 11.09hrs, when Leutnant Helmut Fischer and his radio operator Unteroffizier Kurt Schaefer of the 7th (Long Range Reconnaissance) Staffel of Lehrgeschwader 2 took off from Grimbergen near Brussels in their Messerschmitt 110 and headed for Southend. The clear skies over the south of England had been reported earlier in the day by German weather observation aircraft, and indicated near-perfect conditions for high altitude reconnaissance. Fischer's orders were to reconnoitre the Thames estuary for shipping and photograph Detling airfield.

Stripped of armour and all forward-firing armament except for two machine guns, the Messerschmitt rose swiftly to its penetration altitude of 33,000ft. Once there Fischer levelled out and allowed his speed to build up to the maximum for continuous cruising, 350mph. The German aircraft quickly covered the 60-odd miles from the Belgian coast to

Margate, where the crew spotted a 20-ship convoy in the estuary. Kurt Schaefer tapped out a coded message to base reporting the find. The reconnaissance aircraft continued up the Thames estuary with Fischer and Schaefer systematically scanning the sky around them for any sign of enemy fighters trying to intercept the lone intruder. If the threat could be seen in time there was a good chance the Messerschmitt could outrun the opposition.

The Messerschmitt continued along the Thames Estuary as far as Southend without interference, then swung south to photograph Detling. And, as luck would have it, Detling lay directly under the line the Spitfires were patrolling. For some reason the fighter pilots had received no radio warning from the ground on the presence of the German aircraft in the area; the first they knew of it was when they saw the long white condensation trail high above. Trevor Gray takes up the story:

'We had been on patrol for some time when we noticed a condensation trail above us, heading south. Sqn Ldr Don Macdonell, the squadron commander, took us up after it. When he saw we were not gaining on it fast enough he ordered us to break formation – then we could go after it at the speed of the fastest Spitfire and not the slowest.'

In each of the 23 Spitfires the pilot pushed his throttle 'through the gate' for emergency combat power and headed after the intruder at maximum climbing speed. The relatively tight cruising formations disolved quickly, as the faster aircraft in each squadron began to pull away from the slower ones.

Left:
A remarkable photograph of Spitfires, taken from the vertical camera in Helmut Fischer's Messerschmitt 110 during the high speed chase across Kent on the morning of 21 December 1940, showing a gaggle of Spitfires of No 64 or No 611 Squadron climbing to intercept the German reconnaissance aircraft. The aircraft are flying south-southeast, having just passed over Snodland near Chatham. *Fischer*

Below:
Close-up of an Me 110 of 7. (Long Range Reconnaissance) Staffel of Lehrgeschwader 2, pictured at Brussels–Grimberghen. *Fischer*

Leutnant Helmut Fischer. *Fischer*

By this time Kurt Schaefer had spotted the gaggles of Spitfires climbing to intercept, and started a running commentary on their relative positions. Fischer pushed his throttles wide open and headed south trying to keep himself between the sun and the enemy fighters. In this way he hoped to present as difficult a target as possible, while setting up a lengthy high speed chase which would run the single-engined fighters short of fuel before they could get into firing positions. Afterwards the German pilot reported:

'By increasing revolutions on both engines to 2,500rpm and retracting the glycol radiators, I increased speed and at the same time gained more height. Meanwhile I saw two of the fighters breaking away from the formation and gain altitude rapidly. The radio operator gave me a running commentary of the altitude and range of the pursuing fighters. In a very short time (4–5 minutes) a couple of Spitfires reached a position about 150 metres above me and started the attack.'

At the controls of the leading Spitfire was Trevor Gray, who managed to get 500yd behind the tail of the enemy aircraft. Finding it impossible to close the range further, he loosed off a series of bursts at long range. But the fire was accurate and almost immediately the Messerschmitt's radio operator was mortally wounded. Other rounds smashed away part of the hydraulic system, the aircraft began to trail oil and the port undercarriage leg flopped out of its housing. Fischer hauled his aircraft round in an attempt to drive off the tormentor, but had to break away when another Spitfire swung into a threatening position behind him. With yet other enemy fighters nearing his altitude, it was obvious there was no future for Fischer where he was. He rolled the Messerschmitt on to its back and pulled it into a steep dive, to build up his speed rapidly. Then he rolled the wings level and continued for the coast in a high speed descent. Hard on his heels Trevor Gray followed, firing short bursts whenever he had the enemy in his gunsight. This continued until the Spitfire's ammunition was exhausted, and it peeled away.

Now there were more than a dozen Spitfires in an extended stream edging towards the diving Messerschmitt, the fastest at the front of

the queue and slowest at the rear. Replacing Gray at the head of the stream was Flt Lt Barry Heath of No 611 Squadron:

'I came within range of the enemy at 32,000ft and was about to attack when he dived steeply. I dived after him, waiting until about 20,000ft while a Spitfire did an astern attack. I then fired a 5–6 second burst, closing from 300yd to 100yd. At 5,000ft I had to pull out as I could no longer hold my plane in the dive.'

After Heath completed his attack it was the turn of Flt Sgt Maurice Choron of No 64 Squadron:

'The aircraft we were chasing went into a very steep dive in an attempt to get away. There were three Spitfires in front of me, and we all followed him in a steep dive. Two Spitfires were near enough to open fire. I was following

the enemy aircraft, and got the impression that he was seriously hit from the manner in which he spiralled as he went down. However, he slowly pulled out of his dive and at 8,000ft I was within firing range – 400yd closing to 300yd. I had set my sight for a span of 60ft and fired four bursts with the enemy aircraft right in my line of fire, using 30° forward deflection and dipping the nose of my aircraft during each burst in order to be sure of hitting the enemy aircraft. I could not see my fire hitting him, though I am positive it did so. At about 2,000–1,500ft my safety glass froze up and I could no longer fire with any certainty of hitting, so I broke off my pursuit.'

During the rapid descent from the cold air at high altitude, into air with a higher moisture content lower down, frost now began to form on the inside of the canopies and windscreens of several of the Spitfires. Plt Off J. Lawson-Brown of No 64 Squadron managed to carry through his attack in spite of this problem:
'I only had a view of about 3in diameter when I had cleaned the safety glass with Glycol solution – the rest of the safety glass and some of the perspex was frozen up. I made a quarter attack at 700ft firing one short burst at 250yd range when I was about 5 miles out to sea off Eastbourne. I then came in below astern, and fired two short bursts at 250yd range and closing in, two more bursts at 50ft range. During this attack the enemy aircraft lost height steadily from 300ft to 50ft. With the fourth and final burst of this attack I raked the enemy aircraft from stem to stern by pulling the stick back, and I then had to break off to port and make a steep climbing turn to avoid being forced into the sea by the enemy aircraft. I circled once, but as I could not see anything I set course for Hornchurch.'

After crossing the coast between Eastbourne and Bexhill Fischer headed out to sea at full throttle, dodging in and out of the banks of haze which lay close to the surface. The high speed chase continued for a few miles longer, before one by one the Spitfires were forced to break away as their fuel began to run short. Since the Messerschmitt had not been seen to crash, it could be claimed only as 'damaged'.

Some of the Spitfires had used so much fuel during the pursuit that they were now unable to return to base. Fighters put down to refuel at the forward airfields at Lymne, Hawkinge and Manston. Maurice Choron ran out of fuel near Tunbridge Wells and his aircraft was wrecked in the crash landing which followed. Barrie Heath also ran out of fuel and, attempting a wheels-down landing on a field near Rye, his aircraft suffered considerable damage when it turned on its back. None of the British pilots suffered injury however.

Once he had shaken off the pursuers Fischer remained at low altitude, throttled back to cruising speed and made his way towards the forward airfield at Mardyk near Dunkirk. There he used the emegency air system to extend his undercarriage and made a normal wheels-down landing in the damaged Messerschmitt. The machine had collected 32 hits during the various attacks and the German pilot had indeed been lucky to survive the encounter.

The action had an interesting sequel in 1979, when Helmut Fischer and Trevor Gray met for a second time. On this occasion, however, the German pilot was accorded a cordial reception when he called with his wife at the Surrey home of his one-time opponent. The two men, who had done their utmost to kill each other 39 years earlier, were able to speak as friends on the events of the past.

Trevor Gray (left) and Helmut Fischer pictured in 1979 after they had been brought together by the author. *Gray*

An Air of Battle

Photographs of operational Spitfire IIBs, the cannon-armed version of this mark, are rare. The 'give-away' for the Mk II is the small blister on the starboard side of the engine cowling immediately behind the spinner, covering the redesigned reduction gear fitted to the Merlin XII engine.

Above left:
Plt Off Gene Potter of No 71 (Eagle) Squadron sitting on the cowling of his Mk IIB at North Weald in 1941. The blanket over the rear fuselage conceals the squadron's XR code letters. *Salkeld*

Left:
P8332, a Mk IIB of No 222 Squadron. *RAF Museum*

Below left:
Ground crewman cleaning the port 20mm cannon of a Mk VB of No 72 Squadron at Biggin Hill, September 1941.

Below:
WAAF mechanics helping the pilot to strap into a Spitfire IIA of No 411 (Canadian) Squadron at Digby in October 1941.
Canadian National Archives

Right:
Yellow-nosed Spitfire: AR219, a Westland-built Mk I, was flown as a 'bounce aircraft' by instructors at No 57 Operational Training Unit at Hawarden.
RAF Museum

6

Correct Engine Handling – Key to Survival

In August 1942 the Air Tactics department at the Air Ministry issued the document which follows, as a guide to Spitfire pilots on the optimum engine settings to use when flying over enemy-held territory. Long range sorties had to be planned carefully to meet the diverging requirements of fuel economy, and the need to maintain the highest possible cruising speed in areas where formations were liable to encounter enemy fighters. If Spitfires were 'bounced' while flying at low speed it could take up to two minutes for them to accelerate to maximum speed, during which time they were extremely vulnerable. To reduce the risks while over enemy territory formation leaders were advised to cruise at speeds considerably higher than those for optimum fuel consumption. For a given cruising speed and altitude, different settings of boost pressure and engine revolutions could give substantially different rates of fuel consumption. For example, a Spitfire V cruising at 10,000ft at 281mph (True), with +2lb boost and 2,650rpm, burned fuel at a rate of 35gal/hr; but by flying at the same speed and altitude with +3¾lb boost and 2,000rpm, consumption was only 29gal/hr. Flying at the same altitude at maximum continuous cruising speed, 331mph (True) with +6lb boost and 2,650rpm, consumption was 70gal/hr. During combat, the maximum emergency power setting of +16lb boost and 3,000rpm guzzled fuel at 150gal/hr. A thorough knowledge of which power and rpm settings were best, for particular stages of the mission, could spell the difference between life and death for a Spitfire pilot.

HOW TO MAKE FULL USE OF THE PERFORMANCE OF THE SPITFIRE V, VI AND IX

1. This memorandum . . . is intended to bring to the notice of all concerned the necessity of making full use of the power available in our Spitfire aircraft. It applies equally, in principle, to all our fighter aircraft operating against an enemy whose performance is equal or superior to our own.

2. At the present stage of the war, the enemy in France is equipped with the FW 190, a fighter with an excellent rate of climb and good acceleration. To defeat this aircraft and to avoid casualties on our side, our aircraft must fly as fast as possible whenever they are in the combat zone.

3. In the past, pilots have been told to fly at low rpm and high boost to economise in petrol. All pilots must know the correct rpm and boost at which to fly to obtain the longest duration of flight or range; a Table at Appendix 'A' gives the various durations at different

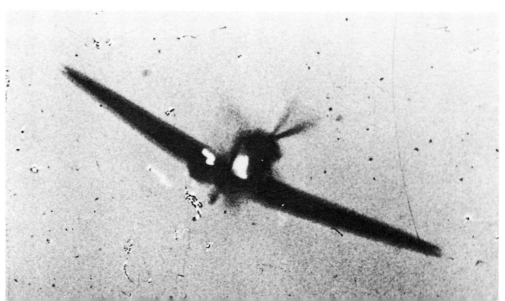

Right:
Spitfire in trouble: combat photos taken from the Messerschmitt 109 of Major Gerhard Schoepfel, commander of III Gruppe of Jagdgeschwader 26, during the action on 27 June 1941 when he claimed a victory. *Schoepfel*

Far right:
Spitfire V of No 234 Squadron being dismantled by a German salvage team after it made a belly landing in northern France in April 1942. *via Ethell*

adjustments of rpm and throttle for the Spitfire VB and VC (Merlin 45 and 46).

4. Wings must still fly at the most economical rpm when they are flying under the enemy RDF [radar] screens but it is essential, as soon as they are liable to be detected, that they open up to maximum power for formation flying.

5. The acceleration of the Spitfire is relatively poor. It is therefore dangerous to cruise at, say, +2 boost and 1,900rpm when the Hun is about, because the time taken in accelerating to maximum speed will allow him quickly to draw into firing range.

6. It is fully realised that the speed of formations depends on the ability of the worst pilots to keep up. This is only a question of training and practice. At present, +5 boost and 2,650rpm are the maximum boost and rpm settings known to be used successfully by a wing. On this occasion, the pilots said that they could have gone faster, and this is definitely a step in the right direction.

7. It is recommended that when planning operations it should be decided at what speed the aircraft should fly and at what point in

Ground running a Mk V of the 309th Squadron, 31st Fighter Group of the US 8th Air Force. This unit flew operations from Westhampnett during the summer and autumn of 1942. *VMI Collection*

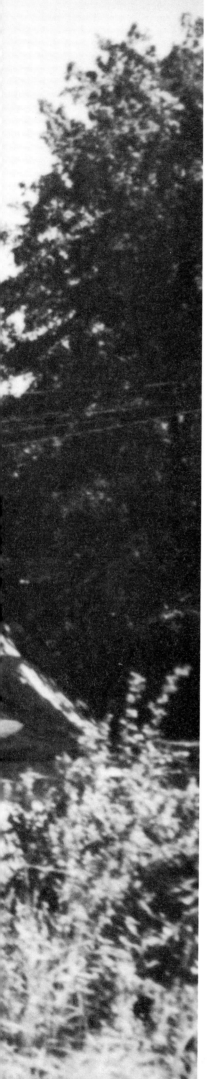

the operation wings should open up to maximum speed. After opening up to maximum speed, they should not throttle back to economical cruising speed until they are well clear of the area in which they may be attacked.

8. Spitfires are now modified to give +16 emergency boost. It must be impressed on pilots that this gives a great increase of speed under 21,500 feet and 18,250 feet for Merlin 46 and 45 engines respectively, and that if used for combat only there is no risk of engine failure.

SAFETY FAST – OR PRUNE'S GUIDE FOR LIVING

(i) Don't loiter. When you can't keep up don't blame your leader: pull your finger out and cut corners.

(ii) Low revs and high boost will bring you safely back to roost.

(iii) Don't wait until you see the Hun before you decide to get a move on. It will take a couple of minutes for your Spitfire to respond after you open up, and by that time whatever you do will be irrelevant. When you are liable to meet the enemy always fly at maximum cruising speed.

(iv) If you want to live on the other side, you must move fast; but equally, if you want to come back again you must save petrol. You will find your engine happier at, say, +4lbs and 1,700rpm than at +1lb and 2,650 rpm.

Both these adjustments give the same A.S.I. [indicated airspeed] but if you fly at +4lbs and 1,700rpm you will save seven gallons of petrol an hour. It is possible to get full throttle and +4lbs above 10,000 feet by reducing the revs until the boost falls to +4lbs. Use full throttle and minimum revs above full throttle height for any desired A.S.I. This gives the best combination of fast cruising and minimum consumption.

(v) When you are travelling at full throttle, and full power is suddenly wanted, it is only necessary to push the constant speed lever fully forward to get full revs and boost. To return to high speed cruising at best economical conditions, reduce your *revs* and not your boost.

(vi) When being briefed, always ask at what revs and boost you should fly. This will naturally depend upon the length of the sweep, but don't forget that:

(a) *when hard pressed* you can fly at +16 boost and 3,000rpm without any danger of [the engine] blowing up,

but

(b) your consumption will be 150 gallons per hour. Study the Table in Appendix A and know how much petrol you are using.

(vii) Finally, when unlikely to be engaged always fly minimum revs and under +4lbs boost; but when in the vicinity of Huns, fly maximum everything and in *good time*.

APPENDIX A
SPITFIRE VB AND C (MERLIN 45 AND 46): APPROXIMATE PETROL CONSUMPTION FIGURES AT VARIOUS BOOST AND REV SETTINGS

A.S.I.	T.A.S	Height	Boost	Revs	Consumption per hour [galls]
250	255	2000	$+4\frac{1}{2}$	2000	42
230	234	2000	$+2\frac{3}{4}$	1800	35*
		2000	$+\frac{1}{2}$	2650	40
200	203	2000	$-\frac{1}{2}$	1800	31*
		2000	$-2\frac{1}{2}$	2650	35
295	331	10000	$+9$	3000	88
		10000	$+6$	2650	70
250	281	10000	$+3\frac{3}{4}$	2000	42*
		10000	$+2$	2650	47
200	225	10000	$-1\frac{1}{2}$	1800	29*
		10000	-3	2650	35
283	368	20000	$+9$	3000	88
268	350	20000	$+6$	2650	70
258	300	20000	$+3\frac{3}{4}$	2650	65
240	310	20000	$+3\frac{3}{4}$	2400	50
230	300	20000	$+1\frac{1}{2}$	2400	46*
		20000	$+1$	2650	48
200	263	20000	$-1\frac{1}{4}$	2200	36*
		20000	$-2\frac{1}{2}$	2650	40
216	335	30000	0	3000	47
180	283	30000	$-3\frac{1}{4}$	2850	41*
		30000	$-3\frac{1}{4}$	3000	43

Consumption at +16lbs boost and 3,000rpm = 150 gallons per hour.
* = Fly at these settings.

PRU Spitfires

Above:
Spitfire PRIC P9426 of the Photographic Reconnaissance unit, pictured after a belly landing at Heston in mid-1940. Note the standard-type roundels and fin flash, unusual on reconnaissance aircraft. Apart from the lack of radio mast and the bulged canopy, the 'give away' that this is a PRIC is the small bulge above the port wing which covered the pump for the 30gal blister tank fitted underneath. The two vertical cameras were housed in a similar blister under the starboard wing. *Tuttle*

Right:
Spitfire PRIG with its pilot, Flg Off Gordon Hughes. Clearly visible are the port-facing oblique camera pointing 13° below the horizontal, the bulged sides of the cockpit canopy and the absence of the radio aerial. This version was used for low altitude photography beneath cloud, when the very pale pink colouring merged with the light background and made detection from the ground difficult. *Tuttle*

Left:
Flg Off Bill Panton pictured with his PRIG.   *Green*

Below:
PRIG R7117 photographed at Benson in 1941. This version usually carried a port-facing oblique camera behind the cockpit; either it was not fitted to this aircraft, or it was one of the few with the camera facing to starboard. Other non-standard features on R7117 are the lack of bulges on the canopy, the presence of the radio mast and unusually prominent markings on the wing upper surfaces and fin.   *Tuttle*

Above and Right:
Sq Ldr Alistair Taylor preparing to board, and running up the engine of his PRIF at Benson. The aircraft was painted in standard PRU blue. The pilot's heavy clothing but lack of Mae West suggests he was about to make a high altitude flight not involving a sea crossing.   *Tuttle*

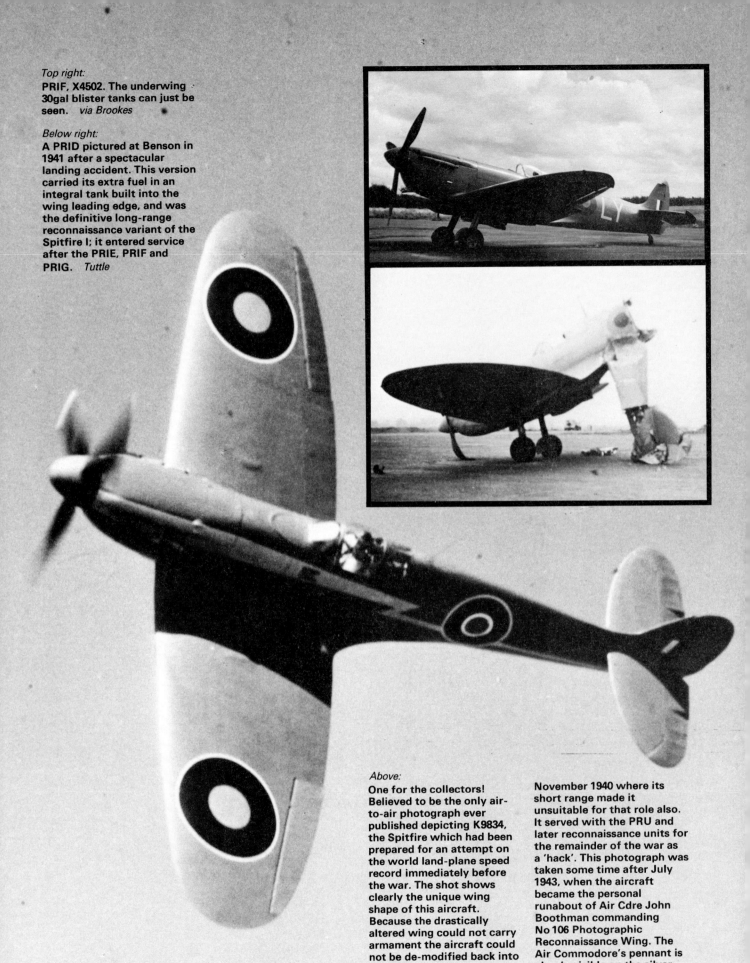

Top right:
PRIF, X4502. The underwing 30gal blister tanks can just be seen. *via Brookes*

Below right:
A PRID pictured at Benson in 1941 after a spectacular landing accident. This version carried its extra fuel in an integral tank built into the wing leading edge, and was the definitive long-range reconnaissance variant of the Spitfire I; it entered service after the PRIE, PRIF and PRIG. *Tuttle*

Above:
One for the collectors! Believed to be the only air-to-air photograph ever published depicting K9834, the Spitfire which had been prepared for an attempt on the world land-plane speed record immediately before the war. The shot shows clearly the unique wing shape of this aircraft. Because the drastically altered wing could not carry armament the aircraft could not be de-modified back into a fighter. It was delivered to the Photographic Reconnaissance Unit in November 1940 where its short range made it unsuitable for that role also. It served with the PRU and later reconnaissance units for the remainder of the war as a 'hack'. This photograph was taken some time after July 1943, when the aircraft became the personal runabout of Air Cdre John Boothman commanding No 106 Photographic Reconnaissance Wing. The Air Commodore's pennant is clearly visible on the silver flash running down the fuselage. *Saffery*

7

Besieged on Malta

Before the war George Hows had trained as an agricultural engineer, and in 1940 he volunteered for the Royal Air Force and trained as an engine fitter. After a brief period with a Hampden bomber squadron, in April 1942 he was posted to Egypt. A few months later, holding the rank of Aircraftman 1st Class Fitter IIE, he arrived on the besieged island of Malta where he was one of the ground crewmen who sweated to keep airworthy the small force of Spitfires on which the island's survival depended. It was a job that would test his improvisational skills to the utmost . . .

'Early in August I was posted to Malta which was then nearing the most critical period of its siege. We flew in by night in a Dakota and, after holding off for about an hour because an air raid was in progress, we were unceremoniously dumped at Luqa and the aircraft made a hasty getaway. No sooner had we set foot on the island than the sirens sounded again. With the other new arrivals I was hustled away from the runway and into a cave which was being used as a shelter.

'The following day I was assigned to No 1435 Flight which operated Spitfire Vs. Just to the east of Luqa airfield was a patch of waste land known as Safi strip, where our Spitfires and the aircraft of other units were dispersed in improvised blast pens made out of 4-gallon petrol cans filled with sand and erected to a height of 12–14ft. Working under a corporal, my task was to carry out 25-hour and other inspections on the Spitfires as they became due. Also we did those engine repairs which were beyond the fitters assigned to the aircraft, as well as engine changes, fault diagnosis and engine tuning. All of our work had to be done in the open, in the blast pens. As well as this routine work, we patched up the Spitfires which had been damaged in battle to keep as many as possible flying. Sometimes the pressure was such that we had to cut corners; bullet holes in the aircraft were often patched over with bits of cloth, even pieces of paper, doped in place. Later we were able to do a smarter job – if the Spitfire survived that long.

'That summer we were desperately short of spare parts and ground equipment. Any aircraft which crash landed and was damaged beyond repair was a Godsend, providing us with virtually our only source of spares. Everything, apart from the simplest of tools, was in short supply. I remember there was only one Rolls Royce Merlin tool kit for the whole of the Safi dispersal area. The only crane we had was a home-made affair, made of pieces of scrap angle-iron bolted on the chassis of an old lorry and incorporating a hand operated cable winch. Necessity was indeed the mother of invention.'

Compounding the problems of those trying to keep Malta's dwindling force of Spitfires serviceable were the frequent attacks on the airfields by German and Italian aircraft.

'At the beginning I was terribly scared by the almost continual air attacks on our dispersal area. But fortunately we had plenty of slit trenches and caves, all of our offices and workshops were in caves.

'The Junkers 87 Stuka dive bombers would concentrate on the ships in the Grand Harbour and the heavy bombers came over most nights. The worst of our tormentors were the low flying Messerschmitt 109s, which came in unannounced during the day to bomb and strafe us. But like everyone else, after about ten days I became used to them. We learned to ignore the sirens and took cover in the slit trenches only when the red flag was hoisted to indicate an imminent danger of attack to Safi itself. As things got hotter the flag stayed up for so long that we could get hardly any work done; so we ignored that too.

'The deep cave shelters which had been blasted out of the solid rock gave considerable protection, and surprisingly few people were injured during these attacks. I have been in caves when they suffered direct hits from bombs, and all we felt was a slight shudder. The main problem in the caves was from the damp, which created health problems when people slept in them for months on end.

'Frequently the runway at Luqa was cratered. Standing by ready to fill in the holes would be a gang of soldiers from the Lancashire Fusiliers with a lorry kept filled with rubble – of which there was never any shortage. An old Valentine tank was used to drag

LAC George Hows, whose account of the siege of Malta appears below.

Spitfire VCs on the aircraft carrier USS *Wasp* during the ship's two sorties in April and May 1942 to deliver fighters to reinforce the defences of Malta. The Spitfires George Hows serviced on Malta during the siege had all flown in from aircraft carriers.
all USN

Above:
Moving up from the hangar, to be ranged on deck ready to take off at first light the following morning.

Left:
His aircraft restrained by the deck crew, the pilot carries out the pre-take-off checks.

Top right:
The deck control officer drops his flag and the pilot pushes forward his throttle before releasing the brakes; already the lift is on its way down to the hangar to pick up the next aircraft.

Bottom right:
Take-off.

clear any aircraft which was wrecked on the runway; it also made a pretty good roller, to compact the rubble in the crater and level it off. Our runway repair teams had the whole thing down to a fine art. It was a rough and ready process, but the runway had to be made serviceable quickly if our aircraft were to be able to land. After a period of such treatment the runway got very rough and pitted, however, and this caused a lot of wear to the Spitfires' tyres. But, such was the loss rate in the summer of 1942, few Spitfires outlived their tyres. On problem after each raid was that there would be numerous splinters from bombs and shells lying all over the runway. So early each morning a detail of about 40 men known as the "Shrapnel Party" would walk shoulder to shoulder down the length of the runway to pick up metal pieces of aircraft, bombs or AA shells.'

At about the time George Hows arrived No 1435 Flight was expanded and re-designated No 1435 Squadron, under the command of Sqn Ldr Tony Lovell. One of the most successful pilots on the unit was Flt Lt Henry McLeod, a Canadian who that summer was credited with 6½ enemy aircraft destroyed or probably destroyed, and one damaged.
'In the Squadron there was a tremendous esprit de corps. If one of our Spitfires brought

down an enemy every man felt he had a share in it be he cook or copper, "wallah" or technical ground staff. Everyone was part of a team with a common cause, to beat the enemy and get back home. Discipline was self-imposed, nobody wanted to let the side down. We never knew what it was to have somebody put on a charge, there weren't such things.

'During the Siege uniform dress simply ceased to exist, it was a question of what one could get hold of. Hardly two people were dressed the same. Often one would see an airman wearing an R.A.F. tunic and Army trousers, and that would be his "best" uniform.

'Towards the end of August the Siege really began to bite, following the near-destruction of a long-awaited supply convoy. Our rations, which had been small enough when I arrived, were cut first to one half and then to one third of normal British Army rations. Breakfast would be a slice of bread and lunch was a ladleful of watery bully-beef soup. The main meal of the day, supper, would usually be a thin slice of bread with some bully beef and a small portion of potatoes with sometimes – if we were lucky – some dried vegetables but seldom enough to allay one's hunger. At Safi village just off the airfield an old woman ran a black market eating house. We had to pay five shillings for a rather foul pancake made out of flour and water, fried in Spitfire hydraulic oil which we had to bring ourselves; and we had to queue for the privilege.

'The worst parts of the Siege were the almost continual bombing and the shortage of food. By November 1942 things were getting very bad, the heavy anti-aircraft guns were limited to a few rounds each day; it must

have been terrible for the gunners to have to sit under cover for the rest of the day after they had fired their allocation of rounds, but there was no alternative. During the Siege we always seemed to have enough fuel and ammunition for our Spitfires, but everything else was in short supply. Motor fuel was so short that bus services on the island had to be suspended. I remember seeing Lord Gort, the governor of Malta, coming to visit Luqa on his bicycle – that was a great morale booster for those who saw him. Very little mail got through to the Island and news from home was sparse and spasmodic. Things became a little easier after a convoy got through in September. With the arrival of another convoy in December we knew the worst of the Siege was over. But it was not until February 1943 that people began to receive parcels from home, many of which had originally been sent for Christmas 1941.'

From then on the air defences of the island became progressively stronger, while the enemy air attacks tailed off to the point where the sounding of a siren became something of an event. No 1435 Squadron was heavily involved in flying missions in support of the invasion of Sicily in July 1943, and the landings on the mainland of Italy two months later. Gradually the Allied forces advanced up the toe of Italy, moving further and further away from Malta.

'In October 1943 we received orders to move to Italy. We loaded our hotch-potch collection of ground equipment and vehicles on tank landing craft which took us to the port of Taranto. We called ourselves "Fred Karno's Air Force". You should have seen our convoy:

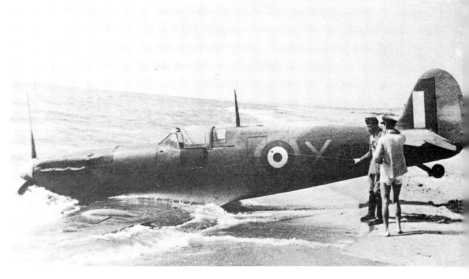

A Bedford 15 cwt truck, an International Petrol Tanker and a couple of Fiat 5-tonners with trailers made into caravans for use as mobile workshops and stores. From Taranto we moved first to Grottaglie and then to Brindisi. In Italy we were expected to operate as a mobile squadron, but no additional vehicles were available. We had to scrounge transport wherever we could. One of my problems concerned sparking plugs: there were 24 in each Merlin engine and they had to be changed after every 25 flying hours. The plugs had to be stripped and sand blasted – but we had no sand blaster. So out came AP1464, the RAF Engineering Handbook, which gave advice on how to make one. We scrounged various bits from wrecked aircraft, including an oil filter container from a Liberator which served as the body of the unit. Proper silver sand was not available, so we used sand off the beach nearby. Connected up to a compressed air cylinder our improvised sand-blaster worked well enough, except on one occasion when the seal blew off the top and the jet of high-pressure sand nearly blinded me.

'There was always a shortage of hand tools, though we were sometimes able to get these from an American squadron in exchange for blankets or a bottle of Scotch.

Top left:
Line-up of Spitfire IXs of No 1435 Squadron at Safi in October 1943, shortly after the unit re-equipped with this version before moving to Italy. *Hows*

Above:
Spitfire IXs of No 1435 Squadron at readiness at Brindisi, Italy in late 1943. These fighters were often scrambled to engage German reconnaissance aircraft, and had been carefully polished with bees wax for maximum performance. *Hows*

Left:
Spitfire V JK707 lying on the beach near Salerno in September 1943. The aircraft belonged to the 307th Squadron, 31st Fighter Group, US Army Air Forces. The official US caption to the photo reads: 'The Curtiss P-40 (foreground) was shot down by mistake by our Anti-Aircraft . . .' *USAF*

Right:
Makeshift servicing arrangements for No 1435 Squadron aircraft at Brindisi. The workshop on the left had been a packing case for an Auster aircraft; the mobile workshops behind the Spitfire were constructed from packing cases bolted to captured Italian vehicles. *Hows*

Below:
Spitfire Vs of No 225 Squadron being serviced 'in the field' under primitive conditions, at Lago, Italy in March 1944.
Canadian National Archives

Bottom:
Mk IX of No 154 Squadron pictured after landing at the newly completed airstrip at Alto, Corsica in April 1944.

'While we were at Brindisi our commander, Sqn Ldr Ronald Webb at that time, launched a campaign to improve the performance of the Mark IX Spitfire. "Webby", as he was known to us all, was a fantastic New Zealander who inspired us to get on with the job with a minimum of fuss. With my corporal I carefully tuned up the engine of his personal aircraft, K for Kathleen. We stripped off the dope (which weighed about 200 pounds) and applied a thin coat of paint over the engine cowling to prevent glare from the sun. Somebody got hold of several pounds of pure beeswax and when the Spitfires were at readiness the ground crews would polish them to get maximum performance.

'Although our squadron was originally intended as an interceptor unit, later the Spitfires were fitted with bomb racks for two 250 pounders. With these they attacked road and rail targets, and shipping across the Adriatic off Yugoslavia and Albania. We felt it was a way of exacting revenge for the "stick" the Germans had given us on Malta.

'We followed the ground forces up through Italy, moving to Foggia and then to Falconara. We were at the latter on 2 May 1945 when the German forces in northern Italy surrendered. On the day before VE day we moved back to a small village just outside Naples, where the Squadron was to be disbanded. The mayor and our CO got together and decided the village should have a victory parade. So we all turned out in the afternoon and marched through the main street, headed by the village band. Then we halted in the centre of the village and the mayor delivered a long speech in Italian, none of which we understood apart from the final sentence which was to the effect that the bars in the village would be open to us for free drinks that evening! On the next day No 1435 Squadron was disbanded. With a total of 150 pilots, groundcrew and administrators, it had been an efficient and dedicated fighting unit. I am proud to have served with it from the first day of its existence until the last.'

Spitfire VIII JF880 of No 417 Squadron RCAF undergoing servicing at Fano, Italy in December 1944.

51

Spitfires with Red Stars

Above and Right:
A Spitfire V of the Red Air Force, one of those delivered early in 1943, pictured at a display of Soviet wartime equipment. The loop aerial above the rear fuselage belonged to the RPK 10M radio compass, a piece of equipment not previously seen on the Spitfire. Because the loop was fixed athwartships, the pilot had to turn the aircraft to take bearings. *via Guest*

Below right:
Spitfire PRIV in Soviet markings. As well as the standard red star national markings on the fuselage and tail, this aircraft also carries one on the engine cowling. Almost certainly this aircraft was one of the four Spitfire IVs detached to Vaenga in northern Russia in the autumn of 1942, to fly photographic reconnaissance missions over northern Norway. When the detachment ended the two surviving Spitfires were handed over to the Soviet Air Force. *via Guest*

8
Problems with the Seafire

The Seafire entered service with No 807 Squadron in June 1942, and first went into action in the Mediterranean the following autumn. It soon became clear that the naval derivative of the Spitfire was not really strong enough for the rough and tumble of deck operations; this, combined with problems of control near the stall and a landing speed higher than previous aircraft operated by the Royal Navy, resulted in numerous deck landing accidents. The Seafire rapidly gained a reputation as a bad naval fighter, but with no other British aircraft available with a comparable performance the Royal Navy had little choice but to use the type.

Jeffrey Quill, the Chief Test Pilot at Supermarine Aviation Ltd, was seconded to the Fleet Air Arm with the rank of Lieutenant Commander to investigate the problems encountered with Seafire deck operations. In February 1944 his analysis of the problem, 'Report on Seafire Deck Landing', was submitted to the Fifth Sea Lord, Rear Adm D. Boyd. The document breaks down the problems into their component parts in a lucid manner, and casts new light on both the Seafire and the general problem of deck-landing high performance aircraft at that time. The contents of the document are included here in their entirety.

MA970 was the first Seafire IIC, the naval version of the Spitfire VC, fitted with the strengthened wing and provision to carry four 20mm cannon or the more normal two cannon and four machine guns. Unusual for an early model Seafire, the aircraft is depicted here fitted with four cannon as it rests on the test catapult at Farnborough.

REPORT ON SEAFIRE DECK LANDING

It is thought that there are four main factors which contribute to the success and practicability of deck landing on ships under conditions as they exist today. These are:–

(1) The method of approach.
(2) The view from the aeroplane.
(3) The 'Speed contrability' of the aeroplane.
(4) The robustness of the aeroplane to withstand the degree of rough usage which may be expected on the deck under seagoing conditions.

No (1) is entirely up to the pilots and D.L.C.Os [Deck Landing Control Officers – the 'Batsmen' who guided aircraft in to land]; the remainder depend on the suitability of the design of the aeroplane.

It is proposed in this report to deal with the above four factors in so far as Seafire aircraft are concerned, with an additional section at the end dealing with some miscellaneous points which directly or indirectly affect the issue.

SECTION 1 THE APPROACH

The success of a deck landing in any aircraft depends very largely on a suitable method of approach being employed. This is particularly the case in Seafire aircraft in which, to get the best results, a fairly high degree of accuracy on the part of the pilots and D.L.C.O.s is necessary.

Broadly speaking, there are three separate methods of making an approach in a Seafire, which are as follows:–

Firstly, the straight approach for some distance dead astern.

Secondly, the 'crab' type of approach which follows a flight path dead astern of the ship, but provides an improved view by pushing the nose of the aircraft away to starboard, and

Thirdly, the approach made from a steady left-hand turn arriving from the port quarter, straightening up to the deck only for the last few yards of the approach.

The first two methods are, in the opinion of the writer, both unsatisfactory. The dead straight approach brings the aircraft straight through a Seafire blind area, which lies some distance astern of the ship. That is to say, when the Seafire is in that area and pointing straight for the ship, the pilot is completely blinded. The result of getting into this blind area is in nearly every case the same: the pilot, finding himself suddenly unable to see either the deck or the D.L.C.O., allows his aircraft to wander off towards the starboard quarter in order that he may regain his view of the deck over the port side of his aircraft, and, by the time he has done this, he is getting very close to the ship and must at the last minute make a sort of 'S' turn in order to

arrive at the deck at all. The result is always the same, and may frequently be witnessed when watching pilots carrying out their initial deck landing training. The aircraft arrives on the deck from the starboard side, following a line of direction across the deck towards the port side, frequently also with drift to port, and thereby putting a severe side load on the tyres and undercarriage, and the back structure as well. Furthermore, should he fail to pick up a wire or break his undercarriage, the chances are that he will go over the port side. Any question of teaching or encouraging Seafire pilots to make approaches from dead astern should be ruled out absolutely.

The 'crab' approach is merely a modification of the straight approach; the idea being that when the pilot finds himself in the blind area he gets round the difficulty by bringing his aircraft on in what is virtually a left-hand side slip, which enables him to see the deck and the D.L.C.O. over the port side of his cockpit. This is all very well for skilled and experienced pilots, but it must be realised that at the best of times a deck landing approach is made at a speed which, in normal conditions, would be regarded as being dangerously close to the stall. The Seafire has very good control characteristics and lateral stability right down to the stall, provided the flight path is straight, but to introduce an element of yaw at speeds close to the stall is a highly dangerous procedure unless the pilot is very sure of himself in the matter of accurate speed control. The accepted way of putting an aeroplane into a spin is to stall it and then apply yaw. Therefore, to ask comparatively inexperienced pilots to fly their Seafire at a speed within a few knots of the stalling speed and then deliberately to apply yaw, is simply asking for trouble.

It is therefore very strongly the opinion of the writer that the best way to avoid the blind area and provide the pilot with a comfortable view of the deck throughout his entire approach is to teach him to bring his aircraft in from the port quarter in a gentle left-hand turn, which is maintained down to a distance very close to the round-down, thereby successfully getting in ahead of the Seafire blind area which lies astern of the ship and which can cause so much trouble. It must not be thought that the degree of the left-hand turn necessary to achieve the desired result is very high. The final line of approach may be described as being from 'fine leg' and the turn automatically resolves itself into straight flight at the last minute, due to the relative speed of the ship to the aircraft.

Achieving the correct line of approach is, of course, entirely a matter of judgement, and can only be achieved by first explaining thoroughly to pupils and pilots exactly what is required and then giving them practice in carrying it out. It depends on the pilot making his turn-in from the down wind leg at precisely the right moment which in itself will vary with the windspeed over the deck and the distance abeam of the ship at which the pilot has made his circuit. The pitfall is trailing; that is to say, the pilot, while endeavouring to come in off a gentle turn, misjudges his approach, arrives lined up with the deck too far astern, thus getting into the blind area, whereupon he wanders off to the starboard quarter, and the result is the same as it would have been if he had made a straight approach all the way. The only way to practice pilots in this is to work them up during their A.D.D.L. [Aerodrome Dummy Deck Landing] training to a point where their ultimate distance of straight approach on to the runway is getting

Left:
Landing sequence of a Seafire III of No 887 Squadron on HMS *Indefatigable*.

Aircraft touches down and . . .

. . . picks up the No 5 wire and is brought to a halt.

The deck handlers push the aircraft back to disengage the hook and unlock the wings . . .

. . . which are then folded manually. *Scales*

Below:
Landing accident on the escort carrier HMS *Atheling* in the Indian Ocean on 29 June 1944. A Seafire of No 899 Squadron missed the barrier and smashed into the aircraft which landed before it, killing both pilots and three members of the flight deck party.

down to an absolute minimum. At the end of his A.D.D.L. training, a pupil should be capable of judging his approach to the runway off a steady left-hand turn, which he should be able to correct accurately at the very last moment. If he becomes used to making the last 300 or 400 yards of his runway approach from a dead straight line, he will inevitably have difficulty when he goes to land on a ship.

Apart from the foregoing remarks, there is another powerful argument in favour of this type of approach which cuts the straight way down to a minimum, and this is that when ships are working in company, aircraft which trail astern of their own carrier are using up too much sea room and too much time. A landing circuit which trails astern is a menace to itself and to any ships which may be operating astern of it and, for that reason, even if the view from a Seafire was so good that it was a practical proposition to make a dead straight approach, such an approach would still be bad carrier technique.

The following are considered to be reasonable rough rules for Seafire deck landing:–

(1) Circuit height – 300/400 feet.
(2) Fly ahead of the ship for 10 to 15 seconds according to the windspeed before commencing circuit.
(3) Keep circuit small.
(4) Lower hook, undercarriage and flaps during circuit before getting abeam of the ship on the down wind leg.
(5) While still ahead of the beam, slow down to 80 knots and watch for moment to commence turn-in, which can only be a matter of judgement, but it will be easier to judge it when you have nothing else to concentrate on.
(6) When on the port quarter during your turn, settle down to your correct speed (70 to 75 knots with a [Seafire] IIC); keep steady rate of descent; watch the D.L.C.O. and your speed and make up your mind that you are going to arrive from the port quarter and NOT the starboard quarter.
(7) If you have difficulty in seeing the batsman, put your head out of the port side of the cockpit.
(8) Wear Mark VII or Mark VIII goggles.

SECTION 2 PILOT'S VIEW

The method of approach outlined in the previous section is designed specifically to provide the pilot with an adequate view of the deck during his approach and landing.

The conclusion to be reached is therefore the pilot's view from a Seafire is not adequate to permit a straight approach to the deck.

If, however, a correct turning approach is made, the view is not too bad.

During the latter part of the approach, however, it is considered advisable that the pilot should put his head out of the side of the cockpit to look round the left-hand side of the windscreen.

To do this Mark VII or Mark VIII goggles are essential and should be compulsory.

Furthermore, pilots doing A.D.D.L.s ashore should be trained to do their A.D.D.L.s with their heads out of the cockpit in order to accustom them to landing in this manner.

A detail which has considerable bearing on the question of view is the type of exhaust manifold fitted.

The triple ejector type with fish tail flame dampers is very bad indeed, and frequently obscures the pilot's view of the batsman. The triple ejector type without flame dampers is better, but the multi ejector type is the only really satisfactory type. It is appreciated that this fact is realised by the authorities, but at the same time there are still a very large number of the unsatisfactory manifolds in use in the squadrons.

However, in general it can be said that the deck landing view of a Seafire is not so bad as it has sometimes been made out to be, but it can be bad if a wrong approach is made.

It is not thought to be a major factor contributing towards deck landing difficulty, other defects in the aircraft, which are dealt with hereafter being, in the writer's opinion, far more important.

SECTION 3 SPEED CONTROLABILITY

This is the quality in an aeroplane which is dependent on the features of its design which renders it either easy or difficult to fly at a steady and accurate speed under conditions of a deck landing approach. Factors in the design which go towards providing either good or bad speed controlability are, firstly, a good degree of fore and aft stability at low speeds and, secondly, the provision of plenty of drag when in the flaps and undercarriage down condition, or, more simply, a low lift/drag ratio.

Now it is in the above respects that I feel bound to report that the Seafire is decidedly lacking. The fore and aft stability during the approach at low speed is very poor, with the result that the aeroplane tends to vary its speed considerably if the pilot allows his attention to wander for a moment. Also, when in the flaps and undercarriage down condition, the machine is still far too clean aerodynamically, and generally lively; if you are going a little too fast you cannot stop, and if you are going a little too slowly and put on a slight burst of engine, the response is so immediate that before you know where you are you are liable to be going too fast again.

Therefore, to maintain that steady speed, steady altitude, and steady rate of descent which are so essential in deck landing, the pilot has to exercise a considerable nicety of touch on both the stick and the throttle. In fact, a degree of skill is required which, while being perfectly well within the capacity of most pilots, is regrettably not to be relied on altogether.

It is the opinion of the writer that the poor speed controlability of the Seafire is the chief cause of trouble with such pilots who do have trouble with Seafires. As an example, the American Hellcats and Corsairs although they are very much heavier aircraft and approach the deck very much faster are, in fact, generally considered easier to land on and it is my opinion that their good speed controlability contributes towards this easiness of deck landing more than anything else.

In view of the suggestions made above, i.e. that the Seafire is inclined to be difficult to control on a steady speed and yet, owing to its lack of drag, must be controlled very accurately, it is thought that slow flying practice, apart from A.D.D.L.s, should form a fairly large part of the Seafire pilot's deck landing training ashore.

Needless to say, the remarks on the subject of stability and drag have been communicated to the designers, who are fully aware of the situation. Seafire Modification No 109, an alteration to the design of the elevator, has already been introduced with a view to improving fore and aft stability, but it is not yet in full use in squadrons and it is thought that retrospective action in introducing this modification should be pushed ahead.

SECTION 4 ROBUSTNESS OF THE AEROPLANE

By comparison with the types of ship-borne aircraft produced in America, the Seafire would appear to be a somewhat delicate structure which is very easily prone to minor damage on landings which would not have damaged an American fighter. This is to a very large degree true, but it must be borne in mind that everything to do with an aircraft is a compromise and there is no question of something for nothing. One of the main principles which has governed development of the Spitfire aircraft is the reduction of weight right down to the lowest practicable limit, and it is only by adhering to this principle that the rate of climb of the aeroplane has been kept superior to the enemies' (and the Americans') contemporary development. What the correct compromise is, between strength to withstand excessively rough treatment on ships and maintenance of good performance in the air, is very difficult to decide. It would appear that in so far as the Fleet Air Arm is concerned

slightly too much strength has been sacrificed in the Seafire in order to maintain a first rate performance, and that in the case of the American fighters too much performance had been sacrificed in order to provide the tremendous robustness which they seem to achieve for deck work. For example, if you cut down the load of petrol on a Hellcat or a Corsair to give it the same fighting range as the Seafire IIC, the performance in climb of those two aircraft is still vastly inferior to that of the Seafire LIIC, indicating that their structure weights and power loadings are far too high to be able to cope satisfactorily with opposition from shore based enemy fighters.

Above:
Landing accident on HMS *Indefatigable* in April 1945, when Seafire S-117 failed to engage a wire, jumped the barrier and rammed into a Firefly and an Avenger in the forward deck park before coming to rest hanging over the side. One man was killed.
Scales

It may be quite rightly argued that the American fighters are required for long range escort work, which will probably not involve them with shore based opposition, and that, therefore, the poor climb performance can be accepted in the interests of the other advantages but, in the case of Seafires which are short or medium range interceptor fighters and assault force fighters, it is felt that it is not reasonable to expect the same degree of robustness and general resistance to rough handling, as the performance requirements are necessarily so much more severe in order to be able to deal with the best that the enemy can put up in the way of fighter opposition from land, and that, therefore, if the Navy have a requirement for an aeroplane which is to equal the best of contemporary R.A.F. development, they must inevitably have a higher rate of damage and unserviceability when operating from ships. This, however, is not in any way intended to infer that the Seafire cannot be greatly improved on in its resistance to bad deck landings, etc., by making use of the knowledge and experience which has been gained up to date. It is evident, for example, both from statistics and from trials that have been carried out, that the present type of splined undercarriage leg does not absorb sufficient energy to prevent damage to the other parts of the structure and that although the new type torsion link leg is an improvement, there is still room for further improvement, which no doubt can be achieved without paying too much in weight. It is held that there is at the moment far too much damage resulting to Seafire undercarriages as a result of what may be termed 'reasonable landings', and that the whole question of developing suitable undercarriage legs, from whatever source, should be tackled energetically.

A lot of minor damage to arrester hooks and to the frames round the snap-up gear, and to the snap-up gear itself, is experienced in service. It can be established from Cine films that the hook snaps up after hooking a wire in less than 1/24th of a second; furthermore, accidents occur at present due to the hook bouncing on contact with the deck and not picking up wires while it has the chance. This was pointed out to Messrs Supermarines, who designed a hydraulic damper to attach between the hook arm and the fuselage. This was fitted to aircraft and flown by me on H.M.S. Pretoria Castle. It had the effect of reducing the force with which the hook snapped up and should, if adopted in service, alleviate the damage to snap-up gears and surrounding frames. As regards the anti-bounce question, this device was tried out by building a ramp across the deck about 18″ abaft No 1 wire, which was intended to cause the hook to bounce over the wire. In every case where the hook struck the ramp when the damper

59

was fitted, it rode over the ramp without bouncing and still picked up No 1 wire. This is merely mentioned as an indication of what can be achieved in the way of reducing minor damage without necessarily resorting to large increases in weight. It is felt that with regard to all further Fleet Air Arm development the provision of a sting type hook, as fitted to most American aircraft, should be obligatory. These hooks are better in every way; in most cases they avoid too much lift of the tail when the wire is picked up but, primarily, they hang down from what is the lowest part of the aircraft and, therefore, their tendency is to pick up an earlier wire than the normal type hook, even if the aircraft is held too high.

MISCELLANEOUS POINTS
(1) D.L.C.O.s
The importance of making a correct type of approach has been mentioned before, and it applies perhaps more to Seafires than to some other aircraft, but yet is still of the utmost importance to all types.

This brings up the question of the D.L.C.O.'s contribution towards achieving these two things. The importance of correct and consistent batting cannot be overestimated. A good deck landing is made by the combined efforts of the pilot and the D.L.C.O.; if either makes a mistake a bad landing is likely to result, but here there is one thing that is important to remember and that it is comparatively easy for the D.L.C.O. to correct a pilot's error, but it may be impossible for the pilot to correct a D.L.C.O.'s error.

There must be very few pilots indeed who would care to try and land a modern type of aircraft on the deck of a carrier without the aid of a D.L.C.O. The landing, therefore, must be regarded as a joint effort, and it is it is essential that the D.L.C.O.s should be as competent and as carefully trained as the pilots themselves. Pilots who are carefully trained to obey the bats reach a stage where they obey them so quickly and instinctively that if the bats make a serious mistake the pilot is very liable indeed to crash. The writer himself in carrying out landings for the purpose of giving practice to a pupil D.L.C.O. experienced the fact that the reaction to obey the bats was quicker than the reaction to query the signal, with the result that he allowed himself to be batted into the rundown, thereby damaging the hook. It might almost be said, therefore, that the bats can hypnotize the pilot into committing suicide and are consequently a most potent weapon in the hands of an untrained or unskilled officer. The following points are therefore submitted for consideration:

(1) Careful selection of Pilots for Training as D.L.C.O.s
Squadron cast-offs due to incompetence, nerves, etc, will not do. Batting is hard work, frequently dangerous, and requiring long periods of concentration and expenditure of energy. A batsman is quite useless unless he holds the confidence of the pilots in his ship and, therefore, his past flying record should be such as to earn their respect and not their amusement.

(2) Standardised and Thorough Training
This goes without saying and it is realised that Easthaven [the training school for Deck Landing Control Officers] have this matter in hand. At the same time it is felt

Unusual company: a Seafire III in formation with a Grumman F6F Hellcat and a captured Japanese Mitsubishi J2M2 Raiden (Allied code-name 'Jack'), during comparative trials flown from the US Navy airfield at Patuxent River, Maryland.   *USN*

that not enough D.L.C.O.s are passing through Easthaven and that there are too many 'quacks'.

(3) Limited Periods of Service as D.L.C.O.s
If the best type of pilot is to be attracted towards the job of D.L.C.O., there must be an assurance that the job is of limited duration and that it forms a definite step in his progress as a squadron officer and that it will not constitute an indefinite delay in achieving what should be his ambition, namely, to command a squadron. At the moment the average young pilot regards, and with some justification, batting as a dead-end or backwater for tired and finished pilots. He would be horrified at the idea of being sent on a batting course because he would regard it as having put paid to his flying career for an indefinite period, possibly for ever. This impression must be removed if the best type of pilot is to be attracted towards a period of service ad D.L.C.O. The ability to be a batsman must come to be regarded as an extra qualification which assists in the career, rather than as a 'stooge' job.

(2) Seafire Wing Tips

Some squadrons of LIIC aircraft have had their wing tips removed and a certain amount of argument has taken place as to the wisdom or otherwise of this step. It is claimed that the removal of the wing tips has the effect of reducing the tendency in a Seafire to float, thereby reducing the chances of barrier accidents. There is no doubt something in this, because theoretically the removal of a portion of non-flapped wing area decreases the lift/drag ratio, which is desirable for deck landing. However, it is thought that the deterioration in the handling qualities of the aeroplane from other points of view which also affect the deck landing when the wing tips are removed, outweighs any slight advantage which may be gained during landing.

Removal of the wing tips produces tangible advantages in:–
(1) Aileron control.
(2) Hangar stowage.
(3) A possible slight advantage in reduction of float.

The disadvantages consequent upon their removal are as follows:–
(1) Increased landing speed.
(2) Aggravation of the root stall (particularly in steep turns).
(3) Loss in take-off performance.
(4) Loss in rate of climb.

It is the writer's opinion that the advantage claimed in reduction of float is speculative; the other two advantages claimed are agreed.

However, it would appear that provided the long wing tip aircraft can be handled in the hangars and on the lifts, there is no justification for making an alteration to the aircraft which reduces the efficiency of the wing and cuts down performance and manoeuvrability in turning circle, and inevitably increases the speed of entry into the wires during a deck landing.

We already know the trouble that has been experienced in landing Seafires in low wind speeds. It has been necessary to cut the diameter of propellers in order to stop them striking the deck when the aircraft pitches owing to high speed of entry into the wires; this reduction of propeller diameter is necessary, but it costs performance to a certain degree. Therefore there would appear to be no logical reason for introducing another modification which further reduces performance while at the same time increasing the speed of entry into the wires, thereby taking away some of the advantages which have been gained by cropping the propellers. There is no doubt that pilots flying short wing tip aircraft have to approach the deck faster than those flying long wing tip aircraft. Only in the most special cases where it is essential to have the advantage in aileron control, should the cropping of wing tips be permitted.

(3) Jettison Tanks

The position of the jettison fuel tank cock and jettison lever [low down on the starboard side of the cockpit, below the undercarriage selection box] renders them difficult to operate, bearing in mind the special conditions which prevail after taking off from the deck of ships working in company. As all aircraft inevitably take off individually, pilots have to pay a great deal of attention to the question of forming up rapidly and in the right formation and not getting mixed up with other ships' aircraft. This has been communicated to the designers.

(4) Airspeed Indicator Calibration Facilities

It is thought that insufficient attention is paid to the accurate functioning of airspeed indicators. Deck landing approaches with Seafires are made to within very fine limits of speed. One hears pilots discussing the question of speed to within matters of one or two knots, but in many cases they have no idea of what degree of accuracy exists in their instruments. All ships should be supplied with the necessary calibration equipment and orders should be issued providing for frequent and accurate use.

(Sgd) *J. K. Quill*
Lt Cdr (A)
RNVR

9

With the Eighth Air Force to Berlin

Right:
Walt Weitner with *High Lady,* **the Spitfire he flew to Berlin on 6 March 1944.** *Weitner*

Spitfire XIs operated by the US 7th Photo Group based at Mount Farm near Oxford.

Below:
PA944 taking off.

Reginald Mitchell had intended the Spitfire as a short range interceptor fighter but, such was the versatility of his design, it was also to prove one of the most effective photographic reconnaissance aircraft of World War 2. Operating at extreme altitudes, reconnaissance Spitfires ranged far and wide over German-occupied territory, bringing back thousands of valuable photographs. A few Spitfire PRXIs were supplied to the US 8th Air Force and equipped the 14th Photo Squadron, 7th Photographic Reconnaissance Group based at Mount Farm near Oxford. In this account Walt Weitner, who as a Major commanded the unit, describes the mission on 6 March 1944 when, flying his personal Spitfire High Lady, he conducted the post-attack reconnaissance immediately following the first full-scale US daylight attack on Berlin. His was the first US-operated reconnaissance Spitfire to fly over the German capital.

A reconnaissance mission to Berlin would take the Spitfire PRXI almost to the limit of its effective radius of action from even the nearest airfield in England. So beforehand Walt Weitner flew *High Lady* to the Royal Air Force airfield at Bradwell Bay near Clacton, where the aircraft's tanks were filled to capacity: 84gal in the two main tanks in front of the cockpit, 132gal in the integral tanks built into the leading edge of each wing, and 90gal in the 'slipper' drop tank under the fuselage. This gave a total fuel load of 306gal, more than *four* times the capacity of the tanks of the prototype Spitfire when she made her maiden flight almost exactly eight years earlier.

Once the refuelling was complete Weitner, wearing several layers of thick clothing to keep out the cold at high altitude, climbed into *High Lady* and strapped in. At 13.30hr, as briefed, he took off.

'With a full load of fuel and that narrow undercarriage, the Spit would "lean" disconcertingly during turns when one taxied. But once you got off the ground and got a little speed she really perked up, she would leap away. Once the gear was up and you pulled up the nose, boy would she climb!

'I took the direct route for Berlin, heading out on 086° over the North Sea towards Holland. Thirty-nine minutes after take-off I passed my first check-point, The Hague, at 39,000 feet. There was 5/10ths cloud cover below, through which I could make out the Zuider Zee.

'The Spitfire was easy to handle at very high altitude. This one was well trimmed and stayed pretty level. One had always to have hold of the stick, but it needed hardly any pressure. In the reconnaissance business you do not fly straight and level for long, you are continually banking to search the sky all around for enemy fighters and check the navigation.

'With all the extra clothing, the parachute, dinghy, life jacket, and oxygen mask, the narrow cockpit of a Spitfire was no place for the claustrophobic! The heavy flying clothing kept me pretty warm, though my extremities did begin to get a bit cold. The temperature outside was about −60°F, and from time to time I would stamp my feet to get the circlation going.

'Throughout the flight at high altitude my Spitfire left a long condensation trail. I could have avoided it by descending below 22,000 feet, but I did not think that was the thing to do on a deep penetration like this. I thought the best bet was to cruise near to the ceiling of a Messerschmitt 109; then, if I had to go up, I had a little margin of altitude I could use. The Germans must have known I was up there but nobody was paying any attention to me. I thought that if enemy fighters did come after me they would have to leave trails too, and I would get plenty of warning.

'As I passed over Hannover the skies were clear and I decided to make a photo run over the city. The intelligence people could always use such photos. There were trails ahead at

PA950 doing a low altitude 'beat up' of the airfield. *Weitner*

BERLIN
ZEHLENDORF
K 1913

Right:
One of the photographs taken by Weitner during his mission to Berlin on 6 March 1944, showing smoke rising from fires in the Zehlendorf district of the city.

Below:
Weitner receiving congratulations after the mission from Lt Col George Lawson, the commander of 7th Photo Group.

about my level, but they were moving on an easterly heading and obviously not aware of my presence.'

The reason for the Germans' lack of interest in the lone Spitfire is not hard to fathom: almost every available Luftwaffe fighter in the area was in action against the force of more than 600 Flying Fortresses and Liberators and their escorts now battling their way westwards back to England, after the attack on Berlin. Over the VHF Weitner could hear snippets of conversations from the distant combats: 'Three Me's at 12 o'clock, 2,000 feet above us. Let's go!'. . . 'One lone bomber down there, shall I escort him home?'. . . 'Here comes one at you, Joe. Dive! I'll tag him.'. . . 'Good show! He's smoking now!'

As the Spitfire neared Berlin, however, the Luftwaffe finally reacted to the intruder high over the Fatherland. Glancing in one of the mirrors in the side-blisters of his canopy, Walt Weitner suddenly realised he was no longer

A PRXI showing the ports for
the split-pair of vertical
cameras in the rear fuselage.
Smithsonian

alone. 'I saw three black forms, also trailing, following an uncomfortable 1,500 yards behind, their altitude just below my own.' The discovery came at a bad time for the American pilot. He was running his engine on the drop tank and from his calculations he knew it was almost empty; but since it had no fuel gauge the only indication when it was dry would be when the engine started to splutter – which might leave him without power at a critical time. He thought of switching to one of the wing tanks and dropping the slipper tank, but the mission required all the fuel the aircraft could carry; if he released the tank it would mess up his fuel calculations and might force him to abandon the mission short of the target. Nor would it solve the problem to switch the engine over to one of the wing tanks for the time being leaving the slipper tank in place, because the latter contained insufficient fuel for him to be sure it would resume feeding if he re-selected it. As an old flying saying puts it: 'The three most useless things to an aviator are the runway behind, the sky above and the fuel he cannot use . . .' Walt Weitner decided to try to outrun the enemy fighters using the last of the fuel in the drop tank, and see what happened.

'I pushed the throttle forward as far as it would go without selecting emergency power, eased up the nose and began to climb. The whole time I nervously held the tank selector valve, ready to switch to one of the internal wing tanks the moment the engine faltered. As I climbed through 40,000 feet I could see that the German fighters behind me had split: one went on my right and two on my left, to box me in. And at that moment the engine coughed. I immediately selected internal fuel and the engine caught right away.

'At 41,500 feet I levelled off and my indicated airspeed increased to 178mph [a true airspeed of about 360mph]. After what seemed forever, but was probably only 2 to 3 minutes, the German fighters began to fall back and slid out of sight. Had they come any closer

65

I should have gone to emergency boost, but it never got that desperate.'

Almost certainly the enemy fighters were Messerschmitt 109s fitted with nitrous oxide power boosting to enhance their high altitude performance, belonging to one of the special high altitude interception units. From German records there is evidence that the aircraft which attempted to intercept Weitner belonged to 1st Gruppe of Jagdgeschwader 3, based at Burg just to the south of the Spitfire's track.

Still keeping a wary eye for the enemy, Weitner checked his navigation and prepared for the first photographic run on the target.
'By now the target was only a few minutes away. I could see the huge Lake Mueritz, some 50 miles north-north-west of Berlin, away to the north but I could not yet see the city itself because of the smoke and industrial haze. I looked around and noted with relief that the enemy aircraft appeared to have abandoned the chase.'

Because the Spitfire lacked a pressurised cabin Weitner had no wish to remain at maximum altitude longer than necessary, so he eased the aircraft back down to 38,000ft. Then he suddenly caught sight of the enemy capital laid out beneath him. The time was 15.30hrs, exactly two hours since he had taken off from Bradwell Bay.
'There was quite a lot of haze, but I could see the sun glinting off the red brick and tile houses. If the German fighters re-appeared I might be able to make only one photographic run so I planned to make the first from almost due north, down wind, to get a good line of photos without drifting off the target. I rolled the Spitfire on its side to line up the string of lakes I was using as check points, levelled out using the artificial horizon and switched on the cameras.'

In the rear fuselage of the Spitfire the two vertically-mounted F.52 cameras, each with a 36in telephoto lens, clicked at five-second intervals to photograph a three-mile wide strip of ground beneath the aircraft. During the photography accurate flying was essential: even a small amount of bank could cause gaps in the cover, and 10° would be sufficient to miss a target altogether. Any correction to the aircraft's flight path had to be made in the five-second intervals between photographs.
'My orders were to photograph the bombers' targets and I had been given aerial photos of the city taken previously by the RAF, with the targets marked on them. But I could see smoke rising from places other than my assigned targets so I decided to photograph the sources of the smoke also. The whole time I kept checking the sky behind my tail, as I expected further interference from the enemy fighters. But none showed up. There was some flak, I could see the smoke bursts mushrooming, but none of it was close.
'I spent about 25 minutes over Berlin, during which I made runs from different directions and took about 70 photographs. Then a solid layer of cloud began moving over the city from the east, and as fuel was beginning to run low I set a course of 297° for home.'

On the return flight Weitner had another drama with his fuel. The order of using the Spitfire XI's fuel was, first, that in the drop tank; next the pilot used the fuel in the wing leading edge tanks, alternating between the two at 15 minute intervals so that the aircraft did not get out of trim; then he was to switch to the lower main tank and finally to the upper main tank. As the last of the fuel in the wing tanks was consumed, the Merlin coughed briefly. Weitner switched to the lower main tank and the engine's even roar resumed. How long it would continue to do so was a moot point, however, for the American pilot was disconcerted to see the needle of the fuel gauge

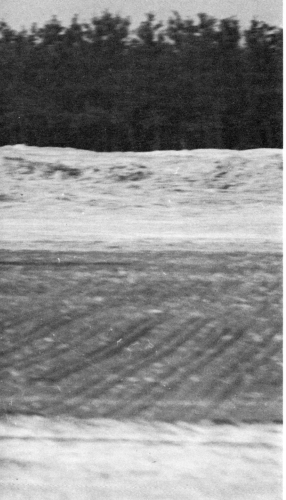

hard against the zero mark. Could there have been a fuel leak, leaving the aircraft with insufficient to regain friendly territory? Or might it be simply that the gauge had frozen up?

'I discovered why I had toiled over maths for so long without learning its true value! Some rapid calculations almost proved the main tanks *had* to be full. During these reveries nothing of a threatening nature showed itself except a few far-off trails to the east. Soon the cloud covering the English coast was within gliding distance, and all was well again. Over the North Sea I descended to 30,000 feet and called "Gangplank" [Bradwell Bay] on the VHF for a homing. Over the coast of East Anglia the gas gauge suddenly came to life showing about 20 gallons. At my altitude I knew I had enough fuel to reach Mount Farm without having to land at the coast to take on more.'

Weitner descended to Mount Farm with the engine throttled back, made a low pass over the airfield, pulled round hard into finals, lowered his flaps and undercarriage and landed. *High Lady* had been airborne for four hours and 18 minutes.

'On entering the dispersal area the gas and the maths ran out simultaneously, leaving a spluttering and dead engine on my hands just a few safe feet short of "according to plan"...'

Above and left:
PRX 1s of No 400 Squadron RCAF operating from Schneverdingen, Germany in April 1945.
Public Archives of Canada

69

A Spitfire PR19 at high
altitude carrying a 170gal
drop tank. *Saffery*

Photographic Reconnaissance

I depend on you, Spitfire, here in this world
Of clear attenuated atmosphere,
The fields of France eight miles below
The sky blue-black, mysterious, above,
And trailing us, the traitorous path of mist
For every Hun to see.

I depend on you, Spitfire. We have no guns
To spit our hate at Me 109s,
Only our wits with which to dodge the Hun
As, self-dependent like a hunted fox,
We set ourselves above the mark
And watch our camera click.

Alone together in the vastness of the sky
The target of a hundred thousand eyes
In each of them the lust to kill
That tiny, potent, speck that's you and me.
I realize now the fox assuredly
Disdains the efforts of the hounds.

by Wg Cdr Nigel Tangye

10

'Anyway, it is only a Short Sea Crossing'

One of the most lonely places on earth is a one-man dinghy out at sea when there appears to be no prospect of immediate rescue. On 15 June 1944 Sqn Ldr John Saffery commanding No 541 Squadron, a photographic reconnaissance unit based at Benson, learned the truth of it after he was forced to bale out over the Straits of Dover. The quotations are from the report he wrote shortly after his rescue. The aircraft involved was RM633, a Spitfire PR19 of the initial production batch.

'On June 15 I was briefed for a target in the Ruhr. After I had got into my flying kit, I decided to wear a new pressure waistcoat which had been given to me to try out the day before. This waistcoat, which can be inflated and used as a Mae West in an emergency, is designed to assist the pilot to get sufficient oxygen into his lungs at great heights.'

The initial batch of Spitfire 19s did not have pressurised cabins; the waistcoat provided counter-pressure around the pilot's chest to assist him to exhale when breathing oxygen under pressure.

'Among other gadgets it has a small electric lamp attached to a scull cap, that winks automatically for 72 hours. When I was strapped into the Spitfire I discovered that the new waistcoat had not been fitted with the quick release attachment for the dinghy lead. As time was short I tied the dinghy lead on to the leg strap of the pressure waistcoat and remarked to the airman who helped me in, 'Anyway, it is only a short sea crossing.' These very nearly joined the list of famous last words.

'I climbed to 30,000 feet quickly as there was a tail wind of 120mph at that height, then levelled out and reduced to 2,100rpm. Towards the top of the climb I looked over the gauges and everything was normal. I crossed out at North Foreland about 25 minutes after take-off. A few minutes later I saw that I was not getting quite the speed I had expected and at about the same time I had a feeling, twice in quick succession, of a sudden lack of traction, rather like slipping a car momentarily into "neutral". I looked round the cockpit and saw that my oil pressure was

reading 5lbs [the normal reading was about 80lb/sq in]. The oil and coolant temperatures were both reasonable so I thought perhaps it was just instrument failure. Nevertheless, I turned back for England an called Manston to say I was returning with engine trouble.

'When I next looked at the instruments the oil pressure was nil and the temperature was rising, though not alarmingly. I moved the pitch lever to the fully coarse position and began to descend. At about 23,000ft the aircraft began to feel rather peculiar and on looking at the dashboard I found to my astonishment that the rev. counter was reading 4,000rpm.'

This was the maximum reading the gauge would show – the normal maximum rpm for the Griffon was 2,750. Almost certainly there had been a failure of the control mechanism for the constant-speed propeller.

'I hastily switched off and continued the descent in a glide at about 180 IAS [180mph, indicated airspeed]. I got another vector from Manston and could see the English coast but I began to doubt whether I could reach it as I was losing height very fast. At about 12,000 feet I told Manston I could see them

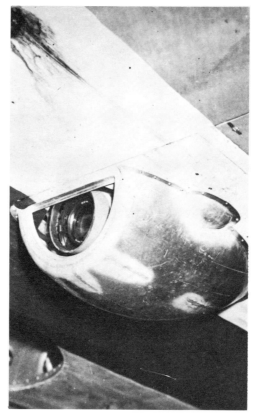

Far left:
Sqn Ldr John Saffrey, whose sea-survival account follows. *Saffrey*

Above:
A PR19 of No 541 Squadron pictured in mid-1944, similar to the one from which John Saffrey parachuted. This early production aircraft lacked the pressurised cabin fitted to later examples of this version. *Saffery*

Left:
A forward-looking oblique camera fitted under the port wing of a Spitfire PR19; a similar installation under the starboard wing permitted stereo photographs to be taken while flying towards the target. A few PR19s of No 542 Squadron carried this installation during the summer of 1944. *IWM*

and asked whether they could see me. There were chalk cliffs on the coast, which meant that an undershoot would be disastrous, and as there was no future in ditching a Spitfire, I called up Manston and said that I was going to bale out. My height was 5,500ft.

'I pushed back the hood, unplugged the radio and oxygen, took off my oxygen mask and undid the Sutton harness [the seat straps]. I saw that I was then doing 140 IAS, so I pushed the nose down until there was 200 on the clock, then rolled the aircraft over with the nose well above the horizon. I let the nose come down, eased the stick forward and dropped out at about 4,500ft.

'I saw the [invasion] stripes on the fuselage slide past me and then looked for the handle of the ripcord. The parachute opened immediately. I saw the aircraft dive straight into the sea and burst into flames. This was reassuring as I thought that the column of smoke would be seen.

'I went into the water drifting sideways, bobbed up again and got rid of the parachute. I then saw the dinghy pack floating beside me. It had burst open on impact and the dinghy was half out. I grabbed the bottle [containing compressed carbon-dioxide], pulled out the pin, shook the dinghy out of the pack and began to inflate it. When the dinghy was fully inflated I remembered that I had not blown up the Mae West part of the pressure waistcoat, so I inflated that too.

'I climbed into the dinghy and lay on my face, puffing and blowing. I turned over to get into a sitting position and found myself back in the sea again. I got in a second time and turned over very cautiously. I then found that the dinghy pack cover had become detached from my harness and I could not find it anywhere. With it had gone the mast, sail, paddles, rations and, worst of all, the rockets and smoke candles.

'As I was rather exhausted, I sat back for a time and could see a big convoy about 3 or 4 miles west of me sailing northwards. Beyond it, about another 5 miles away, were the cliffs of England. It was about 06.40 hours and the morning was warm and sunny with a fresh south-westerly breeze. There was a slight chop on the sea and quite a lot of water in the dinghy. I baled for a bit, threw the drogue over the side and fastened the weather apron about half-way up. I saw a buoy about a mile to the north and tried paddling towards it with my hands but soon gave it up as futile and exhausting. About half an hour after getting into the dinghy I saw a Spitfire go right overhead and guessed that he was looking for me. Soon after I saw two Thunderbolts and later an Avenger which also went overhead. This went on all day and was exasperating. I very much regretted the loss of my signal rockets because I was sure that I would have been spotted in the first hour if I could have made any kind of signal. I tried to use my goggles as a heliograph but without success. I think the search was probably made harder by the sun glinting off the choppy sea, which must have made one little 'K' Type dinghy very inconspicuous. I noticed that the drogue was always out to the port side and was pulling the dinghy broadside to the sea, so I pulled it in and found that the dinghy automatically kept head to sea very well indeed.

'By noon I had drifted north-eastwards out of sight of the buoy, and I could only just see the coast of England when I rode on the top of a wave. The sea was getting higher so I baled 100 times with the baler, reducing the water in the dinghy to about 1½-ins in depth, and then fastened the weather apron right up. I did not put the weather cape over my head as I still had my helmet on and wanted to look about me. About every four hours I gave the dinghy ten puffs of the bellows pump. It was not really necessary but it gave me something to do.

'The Avenger kept up the search right through the middle of the day and I saw him go past me out to sea on one side and then return the other side several times. I was spotted by a number of birds, particularly by a very pretty little tern with red legs and beak who would have landed on my head if I had not upset his approach by moving. There was also a puffin who was greatly intrigued and swam around inspecting me from every angle. He eventually got to within about three feet of me where he bobbed about for quite a time first on one side and then the other. Two porpoises also rolled past but did not come closer than about 20yd – to my relief. In the afternoon the sky clouded over and the swell got longer and higher but although the wind seemed to be freshening it was still quite warm. Some of the seas were breaking and I was periodically soaked, but rather to my surprise I did not suffer from cold. I was wearing ordinary blue battle dress, a woollen pullover, a big woollen sweater, long woollen stockings, flying boots, gauntlets, helmet and Mae West and this outfit kept me very comfortable except for a rather chilly section around the thighs, which were only covered by the battle dress trousers. The search seemed to lower and intensify in the evening and I saw two Spitfires at about 500 feet pass within a mile or two again and again. Sometimes they were even closer. It seemed to me that any aircraft in which the lookout could lie in the nose and search straight ahead, would be a better search aircraft than a single-engined type. About this time I thought of opening my flying rations, but I was not really hungry and I feared that the eating might make me thirsty. I had no water and no prospect of getting water so I decided not to eat anything until the next morning. At about 19.00 hours I saw a Walrus doing a careful search low down about 5 miles south of me. Then when he was about a mile away he headed straight for me and I thought he had seen me, but just about 400 yards short he turned to port and returned the way he had come. As he was very close and only about 300ft up, I was very disappointed.

'The Air Sea Rescue people put on a terrific search and kept it up all day. If I had not lost my signals they would have found me quite early, as they were always in roughly the right area.'

By now dusk was falling, so Saffery pulled on the scull cap and switched on the small emergency lamp.
'Everything was soaking wet and I did not really expect it to work. I then put the weather cape over my shoulders, held the weather apron up to my face and tried to get some

sleep. About 30 minutes later I heard a terrific racket nearby, peeked out and saw an M.T.B. about 30 yards away. I was thrown a line and taken aboard.'

The crew of the motor torpedo boat had seen the lamp winking on the pilot's helmet. Once on board the craft Saffery was taken below decks and stripped of his wet clothing, rubbed down with towels, wrapped in blankets and filled with rum, then put to bed while the boat completed its patrol.

The incident shows well the difficulties of locating a dinghy from the air if there was any sort of sea running and the survivor had no smoke markers, flares or radio beacon. The problem persists to the present day. It was indeed fortunate for John Saffery that the naval patrol boat chanced upon him, had it not done so his chances of survival would have dropped markedly with each hour that passed.

Rare reconnaissance bird. Pink-painted Spitfire FRIX of No 16 Squadron, pictured shortly after D-Day. This aircraft carries a single oblique camera looking to port just behind the cockpit; the cannon have been removed, leaving only the four .303in machine guns as a token armament. *Taylor*

Spit on Floats

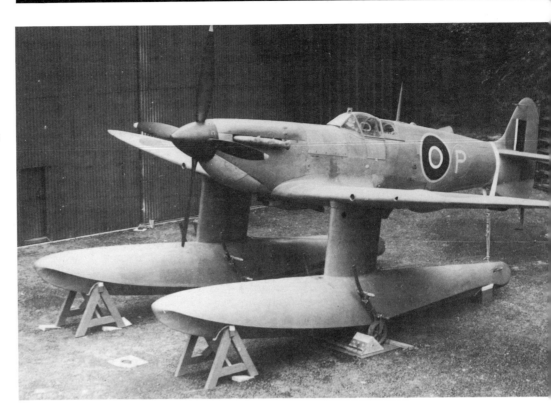

Right:
W3760, the first Spitfire V floatplane, pictured in its original form shortly before it began flight trials from Southampton Water in October 1942. In addition to the floats the aircraft was fitted with a fin extension below the rear fuselage and a four-bladed propeller. The armament was not fitted. In common with other development Spitfires the aircraft carried a spin-recovery parachute in a container at the base of the fin and had a rudder horn balance guard at the top of the fin. Note that at this initial stage the floatplane retained the normal-type carburettor air intake and fin. *Smithsonian*

Below:
W3760 pictured in January 1943, after the fitting of armament, a fin of increased area and a late type tropical air filter with an extended lip.

11

Spitfires Over the Balkans

Now President of the Spitfire Society, David Green was a Flg Off in March 1945 when he was posted as 'A' Flight Commander to No 73 Squadron whose main base was at Biferno in Italy. At the time the unit was flying Spitfire IXs in the fighter-bomber role, in support of partisan forces in Yugoslavia battling with the Germans. In this account he gives his impressions of operations in this theatre, and how the end of the war came suddenly for him.

Although its main base was at Biferno, by this stage of the war No 73 Squadron was one of several Balkans Air Force units which used the airstrip at Prkos near Zara (now Zadar) in Yugoslavia as a forward operating base.

'There was a unique little war going on in Yugoslavia, it was the first time partisan operations had been employed on such a large scale. Although there were no regular forces defending Prkos and there were German troops all over the area, we did not feel particularly threatened. There was a row of mountains between us and the enemy forces and we figured we would have plenty of warning if they tried to advance in our direction.'

Other units using Prkos at that time were Nos 253 and 352 Squadrons with Spitfires, Nos 6 and 351 Squadrons with rocket-firing Hurricanes and No 249 Squadron with Mustangs.

Normally the Spitfires of No 73 Squadron would take off from Biferno in the morning, land at Prkos to refuel, fly two or more sorties from the forward base, landing there to refuel and re-arm between each, then return to Biferno in the evening. David Green flew his first missions in this way on 22 March in PV852 (aircraft letter 'B'). He flew to Prkos, refuelled, then took off to attack the German headquarters at Gospic, about 30 miles north of the airstrip. Afterwards he returned to Prkos, took on more bombs and attacked Gospic again. After these raids he noted in his logbook 'bags of accurate flak'. Later in the day he flew two road reconnaissance sorties from Prykos, then returned to Biferno.

David Green explained the dive-bombing tactics employed by No 73 Squadron during these operations.

'Carrying two 250lb bombs the Spitfire made a very fine dive bomber. It could attack accurately and didn't need a fighter escort because as soon as the bombs had been released it was a fighter. The briefing beforehand had to be good enough for us to be able to fly right up to the target even if we had never been there before, identify it and bomb it – because the flak was often accurate we didn't want to spend time circling in the target area before we went down to attack.

'We normally operated in sections of four, and would fly to the target at 10,000 feet in finger-four battle formation. We would make for an Initial Point decided at the briefing, a distinctive point on the ground in the target area with, ideally, a linear feature like a road, a river or a railway line leading to the target itself. By the time it reached the IP the formation would have increased speed to 260mph Indicated [about 305mph True] and we would be flying in loose echelon to starboard, ready to begin the dive. As the target came into view I would position it so that it appeared to be running down the line of my port cannon. As the target disappeared under the wing I would hold my heading, and when the target emerged from under the trailing edge I would pull the aircraft up to kill the forward speed, roll it over on its back and let the nose drop until the target was lined up in the gunsight graticule. That way one got the Spitfire to go down in the correct angle of dive of 60 degrees. It is a pretty steep dive, it felt as if one was going down vertically. The other aircraft in the section, Nos 2, 3, and 4, would be following me down still in echelon. It was important to trim the aircraft nose-down, otherwise the pressure on the stick would become enormous as the speed built up and the Spitfire tried to pull itself out of the dive. During the dive the speed built up rapidly and it was important to keep an eye on one's height, because the altimeter lag was considerable. When the altimeter read 5,000ft above the target altitude, indicated, that meant the true altitude above the target was about 4,000ft. I would let go my bombs and call

"Bombs gone!"; the other chaps in the section would then release theirs. At the time of release the aircraft would be doing about 420mph Indicated [about 450mph True].

'If there had been little or no flak the desire to see the results of the bombing was usually so great that I would pull hard on the stick to bring the aircraft out of the dive and into a slight climb so that I could look over my shoulder to see where the bombs had gone. But if we were being fired at, we would use our high forward speed to get us down to ground level where there was cover.'

David Green flew a series of similar attacks on 22 March. On the 24th and 25th he flew to Prkos to refuel, then escorted Dakota transports flying into landing strips deep in German occupied Yugoslavia. On each occasion the Spitfire escorts would orbit while the Dakotas landed, off-loaded their cargo and took on wounded, then took off again. During his mission on the 25th, David Green was airborne for two hours 25 minutes. On the 28th he bombed a German position near Otoka, on the 30th flew two attacks on Ostrazac, and on the 31st flew three missions to attack enemy positions at Gospic, Krupa and Ostrazac.

David Green spent most of April on a detachment to the Italian Air Force and returned to his squadron early in May. By then aircraft were staying overnight at Prkos. On the 3rd he flew a bombing and strafing mission against Lipke, on the 4th similar missions against enemy positions at Liubljana and Zelchi.

'We were never worried by enemy fighters. People did see them on the odd occasion, but it was very rare. By this time one felt that most of the fighting was going on in the hinterland. Zagreb, for example, was hotly defended by flak and our chaps did see the odd fighter there. But they never made any attempt to interfere with our aircraft.'

Operations continued in this way until the evening of 6 May, when David Green and other pilots in the Officers' Mess tent at Prkos heard on the BBC News that the war in Europe was over and the German High Command had ordered all of its forces to surrender to the Allies the following morning.

'We had been slotted for the dawn mission the next day, so I called the operations tent on the field telephone and said "Its all over, isn't it, you won't want us to fly tomorrow." Back came the answer "Yes we do, we've got an armed recce for you." I said "The war's over, they have just said so on the radio." And back came the reply "It isn't necessarily

Inset:
Flg Off David Green, whose account of operations over the Balkans follows. *Green*

Right:
David Green, in the aircraft nearest the camera, leading a section of four Spitfires IXs of No 73 Squadron to the take-off point at the forward operating base at Prkos in Yugoslavia in the spring of 1945. Each Spitfire carries two 250lb bombs. *IWM*

over for us. We don't know if the German forces here know the war is over. We want you to go and find out."

'The next morning I was briefed for a reconnaissance quite different from any I had ever flown. With my section I was to search roads and railway lines in northern Yugoslavia leading out of the country, to see what if anything the enemy forces were doing. Our people wanted to know, first, if the German troops in Yugoslavia were indeed surrendering. And if they were, whom were they trying to surrender to? Were they going to stay where they were and surrender to the Yugoslavs or the Russians? Or were they trying to move north and surrender to British and American forces moving into Austria?

'To me it seemed unlikely we would see anything – up till then we had seen very little of the German troops from the air. If they moved it was usually in small numbers, they were very good at camouflage and difficult to spot. Normally we didn't see any activity on the ground until we began an attack and they started to fire at us. For the reconnaissance our aircraft were to carry the normal armament including bombs, but we were not to engage in offensive action unless we were fired at first or threatened.

'With my section I took off from Prkos at first light. I remember thinking this was a funny sort of a mission: nobody could tell me what a surrendering army would look like. We couldn't shout out the cockpit to ask! The only way I could think of to discover whether they were surrendering was to show ourselves and see if they opened fire.

'Initially we headed due east into the brightening sky, past Kazanci and the Makljen Pass as far as Sarajevo. Then we turned north-west and flew along the road past Zenica and towards Banja Luka. With my wing man I flew low up the road between 150 and 500 feet, weaving back and forth with the other pair giving us top cover. There was hardly any activity on the ground and no light flak. It was a clear day, with good visibility and the sun just climbing over the mountains. Below us was the usual lovely Yugoslavian countryside, a bit like south Wales with its moderate hills and valleys and rolling countryside.

'We had just looked at one valley, and pulled up over a line of hills to look at the next. And suddenly, there in front of us, was this enormous convoy of German vehicles extending along the road as far as the eye could see – what in modern parlance we would call a "ten-mile tailback". Some of the vehicles were horse-drawn, they were all heading north at a walking pace.

'As soon as I saw them I told the pilots to increase speed, fuze the bombs and set guns to "fire" in case we ran into trouble. Under normal conditions we would have climbed to height for a dive bombing attack. But now my job was to find out whether they were surrendering.

'We thundered up the road at 100ft at about 300mph, snaking back and forth. It must have looked fairly threatening to the German troops as we ran in. As soon as they saw us a white Verey light arced away from one of the vehicles, leaving a trail of white smoke in the still morning air. Men ran away from the slowly moving convoy, waving their empty hands above their heads while others waved white towels and sheets. The trucks and carts were piled with kit and had men sprawled on top riding wherever they could. Not a shot was fired or a weapon raised, and it was clear these people knew the war was over and had no wish to continue fighting. We flew up the convoy for about 8 miles without reaching the head, with similar signals of surrender all the way. I did not see a single hostile act anywhere. I got the impression that there was a gang of chaps who could not wait to get home. We pulled up and circled the vehicles, and the white flags continued to wave.

'For us there was a lot of curiosity value – it was the first time we seen Germans that we hadn't attacked. For the whole of my adult life, since 1938, I had grown up convinced that all Germans were dangerous; and for the previous six years we had been killing each other. And now all of that had come to an end. Suddenly I wondered "What are we going to do tomorrow?"

'The other pair of Spitfires had been giving top cover, but when it was clear there was going to be no fighting I called them down to have a look too. And they did, we just trailed in line astern past the convoy. When I had seen enough, I led the formation into the climb and radioed back to base the position of the convoy and the fact it was not hostile.

'We formed up in a box and climbed quietly and undramatically away from the enemy of yesterday. Their task was to surrender to the West and keep out of the hands of the Reds. Ours was to return to base – and then see what the future held for us all. There was one small job to be done first. Our bombs were fuzed and had to go. Leading the formation round in a wide sweep to port we coasted out south of Rijeka, past the low lying islands of Cres, Losinj and the oddly named Krk, and out over the clear, clean sea. I put the formation into a shallow 30 degree dive, then we let go our bombs in a salvo.

'I looked back over my shoulder as we climbed away, opening the canopy for the view and some fresh air. The water was already settling where the eight bombs had fallen. We had made what was perhaps the last modest bang of the war in Europe. It was time to go home.'

12

'Franglais' for Spitfire Pilots

The Spitfire brought together men of many nations and produced a comradeship of the air that surmounted national differences and introduced 'Flying English' into many languages. The reader might care to savour the following passage written immediately after the war, by a Belgian Spitfire pilot of No 349 Squadron, in the 'Franglais' spoken by personnel on the unit, many of whom had served with the Royal Air Force for more than four years. At the time of the flight described, July 1945, the Squadron was operating from Wunstorf in Germany.

'Ce matin, pendant que je prenais mon porridge au breakfast, le flight commander est venu me detailer pour un show. Je n'étais pas très keen d'aller encore faire de la line astern ou du close vic pendant une heure mais il fallait bien puisque je venais de rentrer d'un forty-eight en Spit.

'A neuf heures, le three tonner est venu nous prendre au billet pour nous conduire à l'intelligence. Le squadron leader in charge nous a tout d'abord donné une idée du general set up pour le fly past en mettant un emphasis particulier sur le fait que Three-four-nine allait se trouver à l'outside des turns to port et que, en conséquence, ils devaient pousser leur throttle past the gate pour catcher up avec les Typhies de la Six-O-nine, les leaders des sections devaient rester à une dizaine de wingspans les uns des autres, plus ou moins en line abreast car il faisait très bumpy. Le press tits était fixé à dix heures, après quoi le three tonner nous conduisait au dispersal pour un briefing au squadron.

'Nous devions rester tout le temps sur 'A' channel, excepté en cas d'emergency pour un homing urgent.

'A dix heures moins dix, nous étions tous dans nos taxis, strappés in prêts à partir. Au premier essai de mise en marche, mon prop stoppait après deux tours. Je primais encore un peu, mais devais m'arrêter après deux ou trois dopes pour ne pas l'overprimer. Je pressais les tits encore une fois. Des flammes sortaient de mon exhaust, mais je continuais de presser. Press on regardless! Le voilà parti. Il ne me restait plus de temps pour tester quoi que ce soit; le mécano me wavait le all clear, et j'allais taxier out.

'J'arrivais sur le runway quand les autres étaient déjà lined up pour le take off. Je prenais vite ma place de yellow three, juste au moment où le leader donnait le thumbs up.

'Nous voilà partis en l'air. Un virage près du deck nous rapprochait très vite de la blue section qui avait décollé avant nous, mais néanmoins il nous fallait un certain temps avant d'être lined up properly. Le group leader settait course juste au-dessus du lac; pendant ce temps la Three-fifty arrivait balls out to catch up avec la formation.

'Peu de temps après le set course, Red two callait up pour dire que son engine était rough et qu'il devait retourner à la base. Le spare prenait immédiatement sa place.

'Le show passait very smoothly et au bout d'une demi-heure, le Wing est revenu à la base.

'Le break était canif. La red section a breaké immédiatement, la Blue passait en dessous de la Yellow section, qui continuait tout droit. Les atterrissages n'étaient pas trop mauvais à part yellow two, qui draggait in son taxi, donnant l'impression de faire un low level cross country.

'A dispersal, mon slow running cut out m'a encore donné un peu de trouble, mais je l'ai signalé dans le seven hundred.'

Below:
Spitfire IXs of No 349 (Belgian) Squadron. IWM

Right:
A pair of Spitfire LFIXs of No 443 Squadron RCAF, one with clipped wings and the other with standard wings, pictured in April 1945 over their base at Schneverdingen in Germany. The unit code of this squadron was 2I.
Public Archives of Canada

Below right:
RAAF Mk VIII, A58–505 of No 79 Squadron pictured at Biak, New Guinea, April 1945.
Hegge

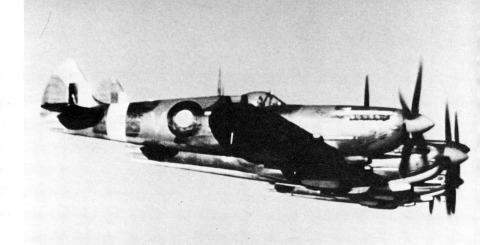

Left:
Mk VIII of No 457 Squadron RAAF bearing the unit's 'shark's mouth' insignia taxying out of Labuan, Borneo in October 1945, prior to the Squadron's return to Australia.
Australian War Memorial

Above and Below:
Mk VIIIs of No 548 Squadron RAF, operating over Darwin, Australia early in 1945.
Glaser

Griffon-Powered Development Spitfires

Above right:
DP845, the first Spitfire powered by a Griffon engine, flew for the first time in November 1941. Initially designated a Mk IV, it was redesignated as Mk 20 before it finally became the prototype Mk XII.
Smithsonian

Right:
DP851, the second Griffon Spitfire, made its maiden flight in August 1942 designated a Mk 20. This aircraft featured a strengthened wing with a revised internal structure. Initially this aircraft was powered by a Griffon II engine with single-stage supercharging. Later it was re-engined with a Griffon 61 with two-stage supercharging and redesignated as a Spitfire 21. This photograph shows the aircraft as a Mk 21 shortly after it resumed flight testing in December 1942, when it was fitted with a four-bladed airscrew; later still the aircraft was fitted with a five-bladed propeller.
Smithsonian

Right:
JF321, one of the six Spitfire VIIIs which early in 1943 were re-engined with two-stage supercharged Griffons to become pre-production Mk XIVs. As well as an enlarged fin, this particular aircraft was fitted with contra-rotating propellers.
Smithsonian

Bottom right:
PP139, the second prototype Mk 21, flew for the first time in July 1943. This aircraft differed markedly from the first prototype being fitted with revised ailerons with balance tabs, revised main wheels with doors to fair off the wheels when retracted and an enlarged fin.
Smithsonian

Late Production Spitfires

LA187, the first production
Mk 21, flew for the first time
in July 1944.   *IWM*

Mk 21s undergoing final
assembly at South Marston
at the end of the war.
Vickers

Right:
A few Mk 21s were fitted with contra-rotating airscrews and delivered to the RAF for testing. This close-up shows details of the installation.

Below:
After the war LA188, the second production Mk 21, was stripped of armament and used for high speed diving trials at Farnborough.
Crown Copyright

Left:
PK312, the prototype Spitfire 22, flew initially with Mk XIV-type tail surfaces. It is seen here with the enlarged 'Spiteful-type' tail.
Smithsonian

Above:
PK431, an early production Mk 22, seen with its original small tail surfaces shortly before completion at Castle Bromwich. *Vickers*

Right:
After the war Spitfire 22s served with most squadrons of the Royal Auxiliary Air Force. These belonged to No 613 (City of Manchester) Squadron and were pictured in 1948 or early 1949. *Smithsonian*

Below right:
PK713, one of the few Mk 24s built. Apart from the serial number, externally this particular aircraft is identical to the late production Mk 22s. But later Mk 24s were fitted with the shorter-barrel Mk V Hispano cannon.

Late Mark Seafires

Left:
NS490, the prototype Seafire XV, was the first Griffon-powered Seafire and corresponded to the Spitfire XII. *Smithsonian*

Below:
SR572, a Seafire XV, landing on HMS *Illustrious* after the war. The Mk XV was the first Griffon-powered Seafire variant, and later production aircraft featured the sting-type arrester hook seen here. In front of the tail wheel was a fixed strut to prevent the wheel fouling the arrester wires.
RAF Museum/Charles Brown

Right:
The Seafire 17 was similar to the Mk XV but featured a cut-down rear fuselage and bubble canopy, and an extended-stroke undercarriage.
RAF Museum/Charles Brown

Far right:
Following the Mk 17, the designation of Seafire mark numbers was revised, and the next version to appear was the Mk 45. TM379, the prototype Seafire 45, was a Spitfire 21 'navalised' by Cunliffe-Owen Aircraft Ltd. The main changes were the installation of naval radio equipment, the fitting of the string-type arrester hook, modification of the main wheel fairings to prevent their fouling the arrester wires and the fitting of a fixed guard in front of the tail wheel for the same purpose. The aircraft was an interim development type and did not have folding wings. *Smithsonian*

Below:
TM379 seen later in its career fitted with a Griffon 85 engine driving contra-rotating propellers. With the original fin the aircraft displayed a measure of lateral instability and in an attempt to cure it this particular Seafire was fitted with an enlarged fin and rudder, which gave the tail an outline quite different from normal. The new surfaces were still not large enough, however, and later aircraft were fitted with the fully enlarged Spiteful-type tail unit. *Smithsonian*

The Seafire 46 was the naval equivalent of the Spitfire 22 with a bubble canopy, though the contra-rotating propeller and enlarged tail surfaces were fitted as standard. Like the Mk 45 this version lacked folding wings and only a few were built pending the development of the definitive Mk 47 version.
RAF Museum/Charles Brown

The Mk 47 was the definitive version of the Seafire. Although outwardly similar to the Mk 46, it featured a system of wing folding quite different from that of earlier marks; on the first 14 aircraft the wings had to be folded manually, but later aircraft were fitted with hydraulic jacks for this purpose. All production aircraft were of the fighter-reconnaissance version, with provision for a vertical camera behind the cockpit and an oblique camera pointing left or right. These photographs were taken during the deck trials with an early production aircraft on HMS *Illustrious* in March 1947.
RAF Museum/Charles Brown

97

Right:
Photographs by Charles Brown taken on *Illustrious* in May 1947 showing Mk 47s landing (not all of the same aircraft). The aircraft picks up the hook and is plucked out of the sky; as it slams down on the deck the long-stroke oleo legs absorb the landing forces. The aircraft is drawn smoothly to a halt by the arrester wires, and even before it comes to rest the deck crew are sprinting out to free the hook.
RAF Museum/Charles Brown

Above:
VP464, a standard production Seafire FR47, wearing the late-1940s light green/medium grey naval colour scheme standard on Royal Navy aircraft, pictured during its maker's flight trials. Under the outer wings this aircraft carries a pair of 22.5gal fixed blister tanks stressed for combat.
Smithsonian

Seafire FR47 on the ground catapult at Farnborough fitted with rollers for the rapid centralisation of the aircraft on the track, in October 1947. The aircraft is rigged for a heavy-weight launch and carries two 22.5gal combat tanks under the wings, a 50gal drop tank under the fuselage and two 500lb bombs. Note the details of the new type of catapult shuttle, the underwing hooks and the bridle connecting them; also the hold-back system fitted to the tail, which incorporated a weak link which broke when the combination of engine thrust and catapult force were sufficient to get the aircraft to flying speed. The photos also show clearly the carburettor air intake extended to immediately behind the spinner, a recognition feature of production Mk 47s.
Crown Copyright

Spitfires and Seafires Abroad

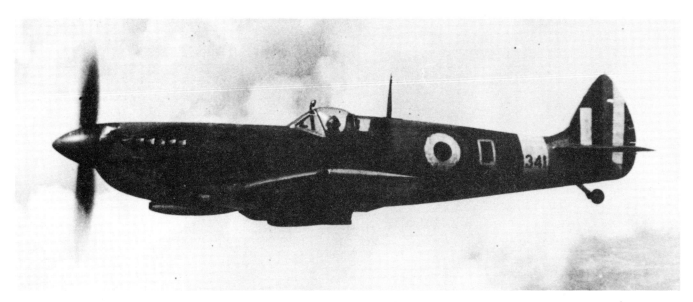

Spitfire IXs of the French Air Force in Indo-China.

Above:
MJ341 of Groupe de Chasse 2/4 'La Fayette' operating from Hanoi, French Indo-China in December 1947.
Goyat

Right:
Mk IXs of GC 1/4 'Dauphine', MJ671 'E' and TD202 'P', flying a combat mission from Nha Trang late in 1947 or early in 1948.

Below right:
Aircraft of GC 1/6 'Corse' at Tourane in October 1950.

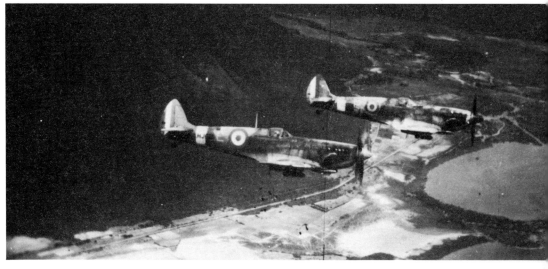

Spitfire IXEs of No 332
Squadron of the Royal
Norwegian Air Force, based
at Gardermoen near Oslo in
1948. Aircraft 'A-CI' carried
its serial number NH193 both
on the fin and on the fuselage
forward of the cockpit.
RAF Museum/Charles Brown

Spitfire IXs of No 322 Squadron of the Royal Dutch Air Force pictured at Semarang airfield, Java in what was then the Dutch East Indies. This unit operated during the war of independence which preceded the foundation of the state of Indonesia in December 1949.

Above right and Right:
Spectacular end of MK993 in January 1949, after it ran off the runway at Semarang following a brake failure and ended up in a paddy field; the pilot was unhurt.
van der Meer

After the war the Royal
Canadian Navy received 35
Seafire XVs, some of which
were operated by No 803
Squadron.

Left:
Aircraft 'H' taking off from
HMCS *Warrier* during 1946.

Below:
Also on *Warrier* in 1946/47,
the deck crew push back
aircraft 'L' to disengage the
hook from the arrester wire;
although a first glance it
appears this aircraft has
clipped wings, in fact the
outer wing panels had been
painted in a lighter colour
than the rest of the machine.
Note the maple leaf above
the fin flash.

Above:
16 April 1947 and a nasty moment for Seafire XV PR504, 'B', after taking the barrier and ending up on its nose; the slipper tank has been torn from the fuselage, spilling fuel over the deck. The crash crews are rushing in with extinguishers to smother the area in foam to prevent a fire.

Right:
Seafire XV PR479 photographed in September 1948 when it belonged to the 1st Training Air Group of the Royal Canadian Navy. It is seen here taking off from Rivers, Manitoba with a rack of 25lb practice bombs under each wing. A non-standard feature of this particular aircraft is the mast behind the cockpit, to support a wire aerial to the tail for the high frequency radio.
Public Archives of Canada.

13
Test Flying the Spiteful

Patrick Shea-Simonds – usually called Shea – learned to fly at the Reading Aero Club in 1934, and gained a commission in the Fleet Air Arm in 1940. Early in 1942 he was appointed Workshops Test Pilot at RNAS Halston where he qualified as an Engineer Officer and was also able to fly every type of aircraft operated by the Royal Navy. In June 1943 he joined No 1 Course at the Empire Test Pilots' School, Boscombe Down, which he completed in February 1944, and was then posted to 'C Flight' at Boscombe engaged in performance testing. Early in September 1944 Frank Furlong, the Deputy Chief Test Pilot at the Supermarine company, was killed while flying the prototype Spiteful and Shea accepted an offer to take his place. In this account Shea tells of his experiences flying the new fighter, and why it was not accepted into service.

The prototype Spiteful, NN660, had in fact been a hybrid aircraft with a Spitfire XIV fuselage and tail married to a completely redesigned wing of the laminar flow type. Shea arrived at High Post, the Supermarine test airfield, five days after Furlong's death and

Left:
Lt Patrick Shea-Simonds, known to all as Shea, whose account of test flying the Spiteful follows, pictured during the war.
Shea-Simonds

Below:
NN664, the second prototype Spiteful, which Shea flew for the first time on 9 April 1945. Later in its career this aircraft was fitted with the enlarged tail surfaces, though it remained unpainted throughout. *Smithsonian*

Right:
NN667, the third and last prototype Spiteful, fitted with an extended carburettor air intake. *Smithsonian*

Far right and Overleaf:
Shea demonstrating RB515, the first production Spiteful 14, for the camera of Charles Brown. The revised shape of the new laminar-flow wing of this aircraft is clearly evident in these photos. *RAF Museum/Charles Brown*

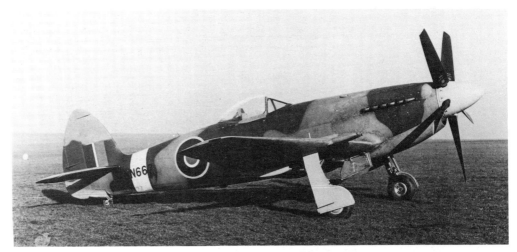

while the accident was a matter of some controversy.

'Frank had been coming back to High Post in NN660 when he met up with one of the production test pilots flying a Spitfire XIV, and the two amused themselves with a mock dogfight. Suddenly Frank's aircraft rolled on its back and went straight into the ground. Afterwards the inevitable happened: the pilot wasn't alive to answer back, so the accident was put down to "pilot error". There was a lot of bad feeling about this amongst the firm's test pilots, it was felt that Frank was not the sort of chap who would have pulled too much "g" and lost control of the aircraft. I had known Frank earlier and I felt the same, but of course I was in no position to comment on the accident because I had not seen it nor had I flown the Spiteful. So, for a time, the matter had to rest there.'

Following the crash of the prototype the Spiteful test programme had come to an abrupt halt, but there was plenty of work for the pilots testing late-mark Spitfires and Seafires. The first task for Shea was to complete the maker's trials of the Seafire XV, before the aircraft went to Boscombe Down for service trials.

In January 1945 NN664, the second prototype Spiteful, was ready for testing. This aircraft was the first 'real' Spiteful, with the redesigned fuselage as well as wings. Jeffrey Quill carried out the initial trials with the second prototype, in the course of which he encountered a problem with the aircraft's controls which seemed to explain Furlong's crash.

'The Spiteful had aileron control rods (instead of the cables on the Spitfire), and these should have given more positive control. But during a test flight in the second prototype while Jeffrey was doing a tight turn to the left and pulling "g" he suddenly found his stick locked hard over. He gave the stick a bash with the palm of his hand which freed it, and after that everything was all right. But had he been at low altitude, as Frank had been, it could

have been very nasty. Jeffrey felt that this could well have been the cause of Frank's accident, and was able to get the court of inquiry to reverse its initial finding that the cause of the accident was "pilot error"; later Frank was awarded a posthumous King's Commendation for his work as a test pilot. After that the control rods of all Spitefuls were very thoroughly checked for freedom of movement, and we never had a recurrence of the problem.'

Shea made his first flight in NN664 on 9 April 1945 and from then on became heavily committed to the Spiteful test programme.

'There were obvious similarities with the Spitfire, but there were also many differences. The cockpit layout of the Spiteful was quite different, it was no longer a "Spitfire cockpit". The most obvious change was the seating position, which was more reclined. Sitting in the seat, one's feet on the rudder pedals felt as if they were "up in the air". Several of the shorter pilots did not like the new seating position. But being 6ft 6in tall, sitting in a Spitfire even with the seat fully down I always felt rather squashed in. I found the Spiteful cockpit much roomier and the view over the nose was definitely better than in the Spitfire.

'The next noticeable thing was that the wide track undercarriage of the Spiteful made the feel of the aircraft on the ground – during taxying, take-off or after landing – very different from that of the Spitfire. A lot of people grizzled on about the Spitfire's narrow track undercarriage, and it certainly wasn't ideal for deck operations. But it did have a curious sort of "bicycle stability" and once the aircraft was rolling it tended to go straight in the direction in which it was pointing. The Spiteful was different, during taxying and landing runs it tended to wander off course and one had to rely on differential braking to keep the aircraft going straight.'

Normally the Spiteful's lack of directional stability on the ground was only a minor irri-

tation. But during a test flight in the new fighter Shea suffered a hydraulic failure while airborne, and found himself in a potentially embarrassing position.

'The undercarriage, brakes and flaps were all hydraulically operated in the Spiteful (on the Spitfire the undercarriage was hydraulically operated, but the brakes and flaps were pneumatically operated). I knew I could get the undercarriage down with the carbon-dioxide emergency system, but I would have no brakes or flaps. Since I had to make a flapless landing I decided to go to Boscombe Down, where the runway was much longer than the one at High Post. I got the aircraft on the ground all right and was trundling down the runway, but as the speed fell away the rudder became less and less effective and the aircraft started to wander to one side. With no brakes, the only thing I could do was give a quick burst of engine to put a bit of slipstream over the rudder and get the aircraft going straight again. I ran on down the runway with a series of ever-decreasing "blips" of the engine, gradually getting slower and slower. The Spiteful ran off the end of the runway going at a walking place, and came to rest without damage on the grass.

'As I got used to the Spiteful I found it not unpleasant to fly. It took off all right and its high speed performance was quite good. To be frank I never liked the "feel" of it as much as I liked the "feel" of the Spitfire, but by then I had a lot of hours on Spitfires and Seafires and they were such beautiful aircraft to fly that it would have been difficult to find anything else that felt as nice. But the main snag with the Spiteful was its low speed handling. The Spitfire had "washout" along the wing [ie the angle of incidence was greatest at the wing root, and decreased progressively toward the tip]; if you held a Spitfire straight and level and throttled back and eased back on the stick, the stall started at the wing root and worked its way out toward the tips. If you continued to hold the aircraft straight, it could be made to sink in a stalled glide with even a measure of lateral control.

'The approach to the stall in the Spiteful was quite different. With the laminar flow wing there was no "washout", and in fact the stall seemed to begin at the tips and work its way in. You didn't get a violent wing drop, but you did get a wing drop and there was pronounced "kicking" of the ailerons. As a warning of an incipient straight stall it was reasonable enough, but it felt nothing like as pleasant as the Spitfire. Approaching a stall, the Spiteful felt as if it was about to do something nasty. On the flare-out before landing, for example, it felt as if it was balanced on a pin and might tilt one way or the other

at any moment. In fact the aircraft didn't finally do anything unpleasant, but it felt as if it might and that was disconcerting until one got used to it.

'Oddly enough the spinning characteristics of the Spiteful were surprisingly good – it was practically impossible to keep the aircraft in a sustained spin. It would go into a violent flick with the nose right up in the air, rather in the same way as the Spitfire, but would often flick itself right out of the incipient spin. You didn't have to worry about taking full recovery action, if you just let go of the controls it would usually come out on its own. Even if you held the controls in a spin-inducing position, the Spiteful would be trying to recover by itself.

'Because of the low speed handling characteristics encountered with the Spiteful we spent a lot of time trying to improve matters on the second prototype and early production aircraft. In due course these aircraft were all fitted with new wings having slightly blunted leading edges, and enlarged tails. We also tried out root spoilers and modifications to the ailerons. The various modifications finally adopted did improve the aircraft's low speed handling, which became noticeably pleasanter. But these improvements were all made at the expense of all-out level speed, with the result that the performance of the Spite-

ful ended up little better than that of the Spitfire 22.'

One reason why the high speed performance of the Spiteful showed no great improvement over that of the late-model Spitfires was that the redesigned wing fitted to the Spitfire 21 and later marks proved to have greater strength and better high speed characteristics than had originally been expected. Initially it had been thought that the wing would run into aileron reversal problems at airspeeds below 500mph and that a new stronger wing of laminar flow profile would be needed if Spitefuls were to be able to exceed this speed safely.

'The idea of the laminar flow wing was very fashionable during the mid-war period as a means of achieving low drag at high speeds. But when it was tested on the Spiteful, the new wing did not give much improvement in performance over the late-type Spitfires. The theory of the laminar flow was all right, but only so long as the wing profile had been manufactured to very fine tolerances and the whole thing was kept free of dirt or minor dents. It needed only a squashed mosquito on the leading edge, and the airflow over that part of the wing went for a Burton!'

With the end of the war in Europe the Royal Air Force lost interest in the piston-engined interceptor: the new jet fighters promised to be considerably more effective and the order for 150 Spitefuls was cancelled. But nobody had yet landed a jet aircraft on an aircraft carrier, and the poor throttle response of the early jet engines threatened to make a missed approach hazardous. With the war in the Pacific likely to continue well into 1946 the Royal Navy had a clear requirement for a piston-engined fighter with the performance of the Spiteful. Less than a week after the Royal Air Force cancelled its order the Admiralty signed a contract for a similar number of its navalised version, the Seafang.

'At the time the war against Japan seemed likely to go on a lot longer, and the Seafang would probably have been a better naval fighter than the Seafire. With the improved forward view over the nose deck landings would have been a lot easier. And it had a very much more robust wide-track under-carriage – during an arrested landing the tendency of the aircraft to "wander" after touch-down would not have mattered. Even with the modifications made to the wing and the tail to improve low-speed handling, the performance at high speed would have been comparable with or slightly better than that of the latest-model Seafires.'

During a flight on 28 September 1945 Shea experienced a near-catastrophic engine failure in RB515, the first production version of the

RB515 pictured after Shea's belly landing at Farnborough on 20 September 1945 following the near disastrous engine explosion.
Shea-Simonds

Right:
Close-up of the wrecked engine of RB515; note the broken supercharger impeller embedded in the side of the cowling. *Shea-Simonds*

Far right, Top:
RB516, the fifth production Spiteful 14, pictured during weapons trials at Boscombe Down. This aircraft featured the lengthened carburettor air intake. Under the fuselage is a 180gal drop tank, and under the wings are four Triplex rockets each comprising of 7.2in howitzer shell with three 3in rocket motors. *Oughton*

Far right, Bottom:
RB518, the sole Spiteful F16 built. Fitted with a Griffon 101 engine with a two-stage three-speed supercharger, in 1947 this aircraft attained a true airspeed of 494mph at 28,500ft, the highest recorded by a British piston-engined machine. *Smithsonian*

Spiteful. He had taken off from High Post for a handling and longitudinal stability test at 30,000ft. Up to 28,000ft the climb was normal and he reduced boost and rpm to bring the aircraft to maximum cruising speed in level flight at 30,000ft. The indicated airspeed slowly increased to 240mph indicated when: 'Suddenly there was a loud explosion and I saw something [in fact a piece of the engine] fly past the cockpit on the starboard side. At the same time the engine began to vibrate very violently, oil began to stream back over the windscreen and cockpit hood. The engine rpm counter was hard against the upper stop reading 4,000rpm – obviously the propeller had "run away".'

The constant speed unit for the propeller had failed and put the blades into fully-fine pitch, thus allowing the engine to overspeed far beyond its safe limits. The Griffon was in the process of shaking itself to pieces . . .
'I took what action I could to deal with the situation: I brought the constant speed control lever back to positive coarse pitch, closed the throttle, pulled the engine cut-out, turned off the fuel and switched off the ignition. At the same time I pulled the nose of the aircraft up, reducing speed to 140mph Indicated. I then opened the cockpit hood, released my safety harness and prepared to abandon the aircraft as I fully expected the engine either to disintegrate completely or to be torn from its mounting. The vibration and high rpm persisted, while oil and glycol streamed around and into the cockpit and I saw a crack develop in the starboard side of the cockpit immediately aft of the windscreen side panel.
'It had been drummed into us at Boscombe

Down that aircraft which went wrong during tests were valuable bits of evidence, and it was the test pilot's job to get them back on the ground in one piece if possible. So although I was ready to bale out, I decided to hang on and see if the aircraft could be saved. After about 15 seconds the rpm fell rapidly, the airscrew came to a stop and the vibration ceased.
'I called Boscombe Down on the radio and informed them that my engine had blown up and I was preparing for a forced landing. By this time I was over the Swindon area, which like Boscombe and High Post was covered in cloud. To the east the skies were clear and as I did not feel like letting down through cloud with the engine out, and could see Farnborough clear and within gliding distance, I decided to land there and informed Boscombe. I had plenty of height and once the vibration ceased the Spiteful handled quite well as a glider. By the time I had descended to 5,000 feet it was obvious that the aircraft wasn't likely to catch fire – if a fire was going to start it would have done so before then. So I re-fastened my harness and started to approach the long runway at Farnborough from the south west. I knew this would bring me in for a down-wind landing, but the surface wind was light and I preferred to approach the airfield over open country rather than over the town.
'It was obvious that the hydraulic systems were no longer working fully and I had no idea what damage had been done to them. So, rather than risk finding that only one undercarriage leg would extend, I decided to land the aircraft with the wheels up. I selected flaps down and worked the hand pump until

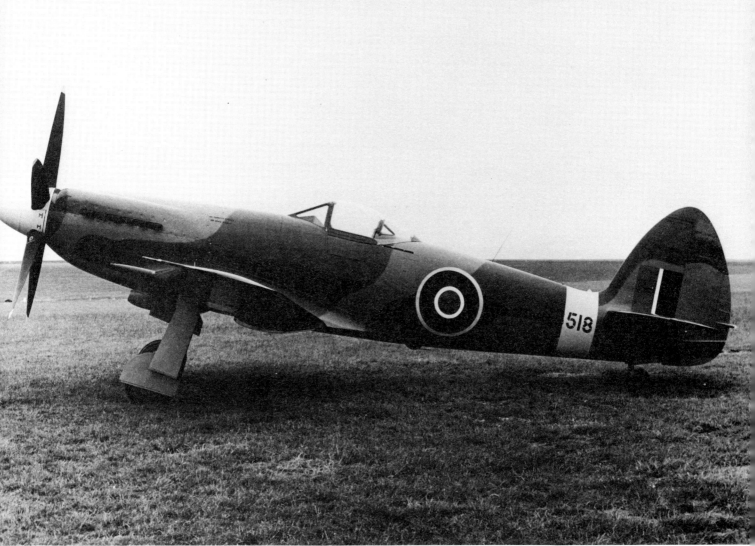

VG471, the first Seafang F31,
was virtually a hooked
Spiteful and carried little
naval equipment. The aircraft
was delivered to the RAE
Farnborough early in 1946
and is depicted following
modifications to the
windscreen and rudder.
Smithsonian

resistance ceased, at which point I had about ¼ flap.

'I made my final approach and landed wheels-up on the grass alongside the main runway. Surprisingly, the touchdown was the least dramatic part of the whole business. The Spiteful had a large wide-span radiator under each wing and slid along the grass on these; it felt just like putting down a flying boat on water. As I touched down I saw the fire tenders and ambulance driving down the runway practically in formation with me.'

On examination of the aircraft it was found that the first stage of the Griffon engine's supercharger had disintegrated completely. There had been considerable damage to the hydraulic, glycol and oil pipes at the rear of the engine, as well as to the cowling and fillets in the vicinity of the supercharger. On the starboard side part of the crankcase had shattered and at least one of the connecting rods had broken. A few days later Joe Smith, Supermarine's Chief Designer, sent Shea a copy of a letter the company had received from Sir Arthur Sidgreaves, the Managing Director of Rolls-Royce, in which he wrote:
'The failure resulted in pieces of the engine being forced through the cowlings, and due to the inertia forces I understand the engine was nearly torn from the airframe. There was also the possibility of fire, so that the pilot would have had every reason to abandon the aeroplane and descend by parachute. The fact that he held on and successfully landed the machine is of great value because it enabled the evidence to be retained and an examination made as to the cause of the trouble, whereas in so many of these instances of failure the evidence is lost.'

Subsequently Shea received a more formal recognition of his feat, in the form of a King's Commendation for Valuable Service in the Air. RB515 suffered surprisingly little damage as a result of the accident and, after repairs and the installation of a new engine, it later resumed flying.

In October 1945 Jeffrey Quill and Shea demonstrated the Spiteful during a display of the latest military aircraft at Farnborough. As the latter recalled, the newest Supermarine product was rather overshadowed:
'Jeffrey flew the Spiteful on the first day and I flew it on the second. The occasion was a bit embarrasing for us, however, because Geoffrey de Havilland stole the show with his very impressive demonstration of the Vampire. It was clear that the writing was on the wall for the piston-engined fighter.'

Because of the continuing Naval interest in the Seafang, and also because the Attacker

VB895, the sole Seafang FR32, was fitted with a contra-rotating propeller and hydraulically folding wings which were to have been standard on production aircraft. Piloted by Mike Lithgow, this aircraft underwent deck landing trials on HMS *Illustrious* in May 1947. *RAF Museum*

jet fighter under construction used essentially the same laminar-flow wing, testing of the Spiteful continued.

'From October 1945 most of my time on Spitefuls was spent mainly in NN664 doing high speed dives – by that time she had been fitted with the larger tail. Much of this work was taken up exploring the aircraft's lateral control characteristics and measuring the stick forces required to apply various amounts of aileron. For this the aircraft was fitted with a stick force recorder and I had to note down the readings and rates of roll on my knee pad.

'Supermarine wanted the figures to calculate the lateral reversal speed, because a similar wing was to be fitted to the Attacker jet fighter then being built. We established that with a generous safety margin the limiting diving speed of the Spiteful was 525mph Indicated at 5,000ft. The aircraft handled well up to that speed and there were no difficulties about pulling it out of the dive. However, this was little better than the limiting speed of the late-model Spitfires or Seafires [the Seafire 47 fitted with folding wings had a safe limiting diving speed of 500mph]. In fact, it was confirmation that the Spitfire wing was a darn sight better and more efficient aerodynamically than had been supposed. And, at the same time, the supposed advantages of the laminar flow wing proved illusory.'

Shea continued test flying the Spiteful until February 1946, when he left Supermarine after having amassed 82 hours flying on the type. Mike Lithgow took over from him as Deputy Chief Test Pilot and did much of the testing of the Seafang, before the production contract for that aircraft was also cancelled

'In my view two things killed the Spiteful as a service fighter: first of all, Boscombe Down took against it from the word go because of its low speed handling characteristics. They were looking at it from the point of view of the average squadron pilot, and had to consider how he would cope with the aircraft. When I was at Boscombe we had to guess the capability of that mythical human being and there was a tendency to assume that he was more of a clot than he actually was. It was not that the Spiteful was really dangerous to fly at low speeds, it just did not feel very nice to anyone flying the aircraft for the first time and particularly so if one was comparing it with the Spitfire.

'The other problem was that the laminar flow wing failed to produce any substantial increase in performance. Had the Spiteful been, say, 30 or 40mph faster than the Spitfire 22, I am sure there would have been far fewer complaints from Boscombe about the low-speed handling characteristics of the aircraft.'

End of an era. Spitfire 22
PK542 pictured in formation
with the first pre-production
Supermarine Swift fighter in
1951.
RAF Museum/Charles Brown